여행
항공
실무
영어

PRACTICAL
TRAVEL & AVIATION ENGLISH

구헌철 이필만

碩学堂

저자소개

구헌철 부산대 영어학 박사
현 대원대학 국제관광과 학과장 교수

이필만 경북대 영어영문학 석사
충북대 영문학 박사수료
현 대원대학 국제관광과 조교수

PRACTICAL TRAVEL & AVIATION ENGLISH.

관광안내 종사자를 위한 영어교재가 많이 개발되어 있으나 국민들의 해외여행 증가로 여행 항공분야에 종사하는 전문인력의 수요가 급증함에 따라 이들을 위한 실용적이고 체계적인 교육이 필요하게 되었다. 이에 본 저자는 현직 또는 미래의 여행·항공관련 산업에 종사하는 전문인력을 위한 여행항공에 초점을 둔 영어 의사사통 교재가 필요하다는 것을 인식하고 교재를 개발하게 되었다.

Part 1에서는 여행사에서 항공기 탑승전 외국인 승객의 여행일정, 예약, 발권, 탑승 수속을 도와주는 실용영어 회화를 담았으며

Part 2에서는 항공기내에서 승객들의 탑승, 좌석안내, 기내식, 영화상영, 돌발상황 등의 안내방송을 담았고,

Part 3에서는 현지에서 입국절차, 호텔, 식당, 교통, 쇼핑, 렌트카 이용 등 해외체류시 필요한 내용을 대화식으로 구성하고,

Part 4에서는 여행 및 항공 종사자들이 필수적으로 알아야 하는 용어를 수록하였다.

그리고 책 뒷부분에 외국항공사 승무원시험 예상문제를 수록하였다.

본 교재를 개발함에 있어 *Ruth Wajnryb*의 Travel & Tourism을 참고했고, 대한항공 승무원 교육자료를 활용하였음을 밝혀둔다. 그리고 이 책의 출판을 위해 후원을 아끼지 않으신 석학당 사장님과 직원들의 노력에 감사의 마음을 전하며 석학당 출판사의 건승을 기원합니다.

2013년 2월

저자 구헌철, 이필만

PRACTICAL TRAVEL & AVIATION ENGLISH

PRACTICAL TRAVEL & AVIATION ENGLISH

여행항공실무영어

구헌철 · 이필만

도서출판 석학당
www.shdbooks.co.kr

Contents

Part I 여행사에서

at a travel agency

Part II 항공기내에서

on board

Part III 외국여행지에서
at a foreign sights

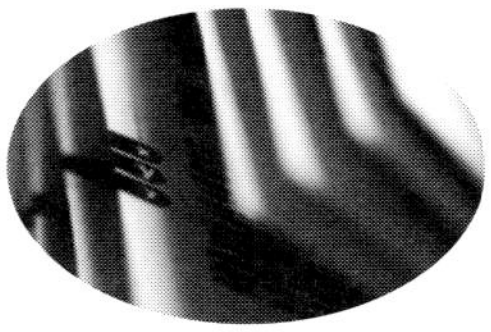

I

여행사에서

PRACTICAL TRAVEL & AVIATION ENGLISH

Part I

at a travel agency

1. 일정표 작성

SCENE 1

Travel Agent : Fine. Do you want to go anywhere else?

Elizabeth : No, just the round trip.

Travel Agent : Oh, I' m sorry, you need to make one extra stop with this ticket.

Elizabeth : Well, OK then.

Travel Agent : So, what city would you like to stop in?

Key Phrase

· travel agent : 여행알선자
· anywhere else : 그 밖에 다른 곳
· round trip : 일주 여행
· extra stop : 추가 체류
· what city would you like to ~ ? : 어느 도시를 ~하고 싶습니까?
· stop in : 체류하다.

SCENE 2

Travel Agent : Fine. Do you want to go anywhere else?

Elizabeth : Yes. I' d like to spend about two weeks in Paris.

Travel Agent : Oh, I' m sorry, ma' am, you can only spend seven days in each city on this itinerary.

Elizabeth : Well, that' s disappointing.

Key Phrase

· I' d like to ~ : I want to ~
· on this itinerary : 이 일정표 상에
· disappointing : 실망스러운
cf) I am disappointed at this result.

SCENE 3

Travel Agent : Fine. Would you like to check your itinerary, ma' am?

Elizabeth : Yes, please.

Travel Agent : Here it is. Does that seem OK?

Elizabeth : Oh, I was hoping to fly through Milan, not Rome.

Travel Agent : Oh, I' m very sorry, ma' am. I' ll change that right away.

Key Phrase

· check : 점검(대조)하다, (명)수표
· Here it is : 여기 있습니다.(= Here you are.)
· fly : 비행기를 타다.
· right away : 즉시(=right now)

SCENE 4

Travel Agent : Fine, Is there anything else you' d like?

Elizabeth : I' d like to sit in a non–smoking section of the plane.

Travel Agent : You need to tell them that when you check in at the airport.

Elizabeth : OK, thank you.

Travel Agent : It' s my pleasure.

Key Phrase

· Is there anything else : 그밖에 다른 것이 있습니까?
· non–smoking section : 비흡연 구역
  cf) ↔ smoking section : 흡연구역
· check in : 대조하다.
· It' s my pleasure : 별 말씀을.

[Situation] Elizabeth walks into a travel agency.

Elizabeth : Hello. I' m planning a trip to London. I' d like to get some information, please.

Travel agent : Sure, When do you plan to go?

Elizabeth : Well, I' d like to be there next month.

Travel agent : OK. And how long do you want to stay in London?

Elizabeth : About a week.

Travel agent : Fine. Do you want to go anywhere else?

Elizabeth : Yes, I' d like to make a few stops in Europe.

Travel agent : OK, sure. There' s a Eurotrip package that gives you a round trip to London and then three stops in Europe.

Elizabeth : Can I choose the stops?

Travel agent : Certainly. Tell me where you' d like to stop off and we can print out an itinerary for you.

Elizabeth : Thank you very much for your help.

Key Phrase

· I' m planning a trip to~ : ~로 여행할 계획입니다.
· get some information : 정보를 좀 얻다.
· how long do you want to stay? : 얼마나 (오래) 머무실 겁니까?
· make a few stops : 몇 군데 체류하다.
· Eurotrip package : 유럽여행 패키지
· Certainly : 물론입니다.
· Tell me where~ : 어디에 ~할 건지 말씀해 주십시오.
· print out : 출력하다.
· Thank you for ~ : ~에 감사드립니다.

2. 비행편 예약

SCENE 1

Travel Agent : I' ll have a look at what' s available. It shouldn' t be too difficult... Oh, I' m sorry, the Ansett flight is full.

Elizabeth : Can you see if there are any others arriving at the same time?

Travel Agent : Yes, of course... I' m sorry, but they' re all full. Do you want me to put you on the waiting list?

Elizabeth : Yes, please.

Key Phrase

- I' ll have a look at ~ : ~을 한 번 보겠습니다.
- what' s available : 어떤 것이 가능한 지
- It shouldn' t be too difficult : 그것은 결코 어렵지 않습니다.
- the Ansett flight is full : 안세트 비행편은 만원입니다.
- Can you see if ~ ? : ~인지 어떤지 알 수 있겠습니까?
- at the same time : 동시에
- put on the waiting list : 대기 목록에 올려놓다.

SCENE 2

Travel Agent : I' ll have a look at what' s available. It shouldn' t be too difficult... Yes, there are seats available on this flight, but they' re in business class, not economy.

Elizabeth : What' s the difference in price?

Travel Agent : Business class is about twice the price.

Elizabeth : Well, um. can you reserve one for me?

Key Phrase

- seats available : 이용가능한(비어있는) 좌석
- business class : 특별석 (↔ economy class : 보통석)
- What' s the difference in price? : 가격 차이는 어떻습니까?
- about twice the price : 그 가격의 약 두배

SCENE 3

Travel Agent : I' ll have a look at what' s available. It shouldn' t be too difficult... Oh, dear, the computer is down. I can' t check that flight right now.

Elizabeth : How long do I have to wait?

Travel Agent : I' m sure it will be working soon. I' m very sorry, ma' am.

Key Phrase

· the computer is down : 컴퓨터가 다운되다.
· How long do I have to wait? : 얼나마 기다려야 하나요?
· I' m sure ~ : ~을 확신합니다.
· work : (기계가) 작동하다.

SCENE 4

Travel Agent : I' ll have a look at what' s available. It shouldn' t be too difficult... There are actually two flights which leave on Friday. One is direct, but it lands at 2 A.M.

Elizabeth : I... I... I think I' d prefer to arrive later.

Travel Agent : So, can I reserve the later flight for you?

Elizabeth : Yes, please.

Key Phrase

· actually : 실제로
· flight : 비행기, 비행편
· direct : 직행, 직접적인
· land : 착륙하다.
· prefer : 선호하다(더 좋아하다).
cf) I prefer to die than to live in disgrace.
· reserve : 예약하다.

[Situation] Elizabeth walks into a travel agency in Tokyo.

Travel Agent : Can I help you?

Elizabeth : Ah, yes. I want to arrange a one-way flight to Sydney, Australia, arriving on Saturday.

Travel Agent : OK. Is that just for one person?

Elizabeth : Yes, economy class, please.

Travel Agent : Yes, there's an Ansett flight that leaves on Friday night and lands in Sydney on Saturday at 6 A.M. I can get you a seat on that one. Is that all right?

Elizabeth : Yes, that'd be perfect. Can you arrange it for me, please?

Travel Agent : Sure, Do you want to pay for it now?

Elizabeth : Yes, thank you.

Key Phrase

· arrange : 예약하다, 준비하다
· one-way flight : 편도 비행(↔ round-trip flight)
· I can get you a seat : 좌석을 구해 드릴 수 있습니다
· that'd be perfect : 더 할 나위없이 좋습니다
= that wouldn't be better
cf) perfect : 완벽한
· pay for ~ : ~의 값을 지불하다
cf) pay + 비용, pay for + 물건

3. 호텔 예약

SCENE 1

Travel Agent : The Imperial' s a three-star hotel in the city with views of the Opera House.

Elizabeth : Does it have rooms for 100 dollars a night?

Travel Agent : Yes, there are budget rooms on the lower floors, but you have to share a bathroom with other guests.

Elizabeth : Well, I... I guess that' s all right.

Travel Agent : Shall I reserve one for you, ma' am?

Elizabeth : Yes, please.

Key Phrase

· three-star hotel : 삼(三)성(星) 호텔
· with views of ~ : ~의 경치가 보이는
· budget room : 값싼 방 cf) budget : 예산
· share : 나누어 쓰다.

SCENE 2

Travel Agent : The Imperial' s a three-star hotel in the city with views of the Opera House.

Elizabeth : Great. I' d like a room with a view for about 150 per night.

Travel Agent : I' m sorry, that' s not possible. Rooms with a view start at 250 dollars a night.

Elizabeth : What about another hotel, then?

Travel Agent : OK, let' s have a look.

Key Phrase

· 150 per night : 하루밤에 150달러
· What about ~? : ~을 어떻게 생각하십니까?
= What do you think about ~?

SCENE 3

Travel Agent : The Imperial' s a three-star hotel in the city with views of the Opera House.

Elizabeth : Well, can I have a room at 250 dollars for five nights, starting Saturday?

Travel Agent : I' m sorry, I can only offer you a room at that price for three nights.

Elizabeth : Oh, what a shame! Well, I' ll take it for three nights.

Travel Agent : Very well, ma' am.

Key Phrase

- offer : 제공하다, 주다.
- at that price : 그 가격으로
- what a shame! : 너무하군요!
- I' ll take it : 그것을 선택하겠습니다.

SCENE 4

Travel Agent : The Imperial' s a three-star hotel in the city with views of the Opera House.

Elizabeth : That sounds like what I want. Can you reserve a room there for five nights?

Travel Agent : Sure, no problem. The rooms are 200 a night.

Elizabeth : Fine. There aren' t any extra charges, are there?

Travel Agent : Just the reservation fee – that' s 20 dollars.

Elizabeth : Well, OK.

Key Phrase

- That sounds like what I want : 그것은 내가 원하던 바이군요.
- extra charges : 추가 비용
- reservation fee : 예약금

[Situation] Elizabeth is at a travel agency discussing her trip to Seattle, USA.

Travel Agent : Have you organized accommodation?

Elizabeth : No, I haven' t yet. Can you help me with that?

Travel Agent : Sure. I' ll need to know what you have in mind. Have you ever visited Seattle?

Elizabeth : No, I haven' t. I' d like to be downtown, but I don' t want to pay a lot.

Travel Agent : OK, the Stanton' s a three-star hotel right in the city with views of the water. The room prices range from 150 to 300 dollars a night.

Elizabeth : Well, I don' t really need a view. Can I have something for 150?

Travel Agent : Yes, there are very nice rooms on the lower floors at that price. Shall I reserve one for you?

Elizabeth : Yes, thank you. I want to stay for five nights, please.

Travel Agent : Fine, no problem.

Key Phrase

· organize accommodation : 숙박지를 정하다.
  (organize 구성하다, accommodation 숙박시설)
· what you have in mind : 당신이 마음에 두고 있는 것
· Have you ever p.p.~? : ~을 하신 적이 있습니까?
· a lot : 많이
· with views of the water : 물(의 경치가)이 보이는
· range from ~ to … : (범위가) ~에서 …까지 입니다.
· the lower floor : 더 낮은 층
· Shall I reserve one for you? : (손님을 위해) 예약을 해드릴까요?

4. 탑승 절차

SCENE 1

Ground Staff : Is it one bag only? The small one – that' s your carry on?

Elizabeth : Yes, that' s right.

Ground Staff : I' m sorry, ma' am, this bag is over 70 pounds. You' re actually over the limit.

Elizabeth : Oh no, I was afraid of that. Should I pay for that now?

Ground Staff : Yes, please.

Key Phrase

- ground staff : 지상근무 요원
- carry on : 휴대하다.
- over the limit : 한계를 넘어선
- I was afraid of that : 유감입니다.
- Should I pay for that? : 그 값을 지불해야 하나요?

SCENE 2

Ground Staff : Is it one bag only? The small one – that' s your carry on?

Elizabeth : Yes, that' s right.

Ground Staff : Oh, dear, did you check the size? It' s larger than the regulations allow, ma' am. I' m sorry, but you' ll have to check it in with the big one.

Elizabeth : Oh, do I have to? But there are things in that I' ll need on the plane.

Ground Staff : You can take out whatever you like, ma' am, before I check it in.

Key Phrase

- It' s larger than the regulations allow : 규정보다 더 크군요.
- take out : 끄집어 내다.
- whatever you like : 원하시는 어떤 것이라도.

SCENE 3

Ground Staff : Could I have your ticket and passport, please?

Elizabeth : Here you are.

Ground Staff : Thank you... Oh, what' s this? This ticket is for the same flight tomorrow.

Elizabeth : Oh no! I really have to go today. Can you change the ticket?

Ground Staff : Yes, this ticket can be changed. I' ll have a look at the seats for you... Yes, you' re in luck!

Key Phrase

· Could I have ~? : ~을 보여주시겠습니까?
  = May I have ~? = Please show me ~?
· Here you are : 여기 있습니다.
· I' ll have a look at the seats for you : 좌석을 알아봐 드리겠습니다.
  = Let me look at the seats for you
· you' re in luck

SCENE 4

Ground Staff : Could I have your ticket and passport, please?

Elizabeth : Here you are.

Ground Staff : Your ticket has a further connection to Bangkok.

Elizabeth : Bangkok? It...it should be Singapore!

Ground Staff : OK, this shouldn' t be a problem. I' ll just change your ticket for you.

Key Phrase

· a further connection : 연장 연결비행편
  further : 더 멀리
  connection : 연결비행편

[Situation] Elizabeth arrives at the check-in desk at the airport. She has two bags with her.

Ground Staff : Good morning, ma' am. How are you and where are you traveling to this morning?

Elizabeth : Good morning. I' m fine, thank you. I' m off to Jakarta.

Ground Staff : Your ticket and passport, please.

Elizabeth : Here you are.

Ground Staff : How many bags do you have?

Elizabeth : This one to check in and a small one to carry on.

Ground Staff : Your ticket has a further connection to Bangkok and then a return connection from there.

Elizabeth : Yes, I' m doing some business in Jakarta and I' m meeting up with my husband in Bangkok for a vacation.

Ground Staff : Well, this is a beautiful time of year for it, ma' am. OK then, your flight Ansett 17 to Jakarta leaves at 11:15 from Gate 5 and you' ll hear the first boarding call. Have a good trip.

Elizabeth : Thank you very much.

Key Phrase

· check-in desk : 접수대
· I' m off to ~ : ~로 떠날겁니다
· How many bags do you have? : 가방을 몇 개 가지고 있습니까?
· a return connection : 귀국 연결비행편
· a beautiful time of year : 연중 아름다운 때
· Gate 5 : 5번 출구
cf) Round 3 : 3회전
· boarding pass : 탑승권
· Have a good trip : 좋은 여행 보내십시오.

5. 착륙 정보

SCENE 1

Elizabeth : Can you tell me how long I have to wait for the connection?

Ground Staff : Only about 45 minutes.

Elizabeth : Only 45 minutes! That' s not much time. I was hoping to do some duty-free shopping at the airport.

Ground Staff : You might have more luck on the return flight.

Key Phrase

- Can you tell me how long ~? : 얼마나 ~할 지 말씀해 주시겠습니까?
- connection : 연결비행편
- duty-free shop : 면세점
- You might have more luck on the return flight : 귀국 비행편에 더 많은 행운을 잡을 수 있습니다.

SCENE 2

Elizabeth : Can you tell me what time the plane lands in Paris?

Ground Staff : Yes, it gets to Charles de Gaulle at 6 P.M.

Elizabeth : I thought it landed at about seven o' clock?

Ground Staff : No, this flight arrives at 6 P.M.

Key Phrase

- Can you tell me what time ~? : 몇 시에 ~하는지 말씀해 주시겠습니까?
- land : 착륙하다.
- get to : 도착하다(arrive at).
- I think ~ : 내 생각에는 ~

SCENE 3

Elizabeth : Can you tell me if I have to claim my luggage during the stopover?

Ground Staff : Yes, you will have to claim it because the connecting flight is a domestic one.

Elizabeth : That' s annoying. My bag' s very heavy.

Ground Staff : You should be able to get a cart at the airport.

Key Phrase

· Can you tell me if ~? : ~인지 어떤지 말씀해 주십시오.
· claim luggage : 짐을 찾다(수화물을 청구하다).
· stopover : 중간체류
· connecting flight : 연결 비행편
· domestic : 국내선 (↔ 국제선 foreign)
· annoying : 성가신
· cart : 짐수레

SCENE 4

Elizabeth : Can you tell me what time the flight arrives?

Ground Staff : Yes, at 1800 hours.

Elizabeth : What does that mean? Is it in the morning or in the evening?

Ground Staff : It' s 6 P.M. in the evening, ma' am.

Elizabeth : Thank you.

Key Phrase

· What does that mean? : 그게 무슨 말이죠?

[Situation] Elizabeth is at the airport check-in counter.

Ground Staff : Your plane leaves from Gate 5 at 2:15. Take the escalator over there to the next floor where you' ll go through the security check.

Elizabeth : Thank you. Could you tell me what time the flight arrives in Paris?

Ground Staff : Yes, it gets to Charles de Gaulle at six o' clock in the evening. That' s local time.

Elizabeth : OK. What about the stopover in Bangkok? I' d like to know how long I have to wait for the connection.

Ground Staff : You land a Bangkok at 10:00 A.M. and your connecting flight is at 1:00. So that' s about three hours in transit.

Elizabeth : Can you tell me if I have to claim my luggage at the Bangkok air-port?

Ground Staff : You won' t have to worry about your luggage until you get to Paris.

Elizabeth : That' s great!

Key Phrase

· take escalator : 자동계단을 타다.
· security check : 보안검색대
· get to : 도착하다.
· local time : 현지시간
· I' d like to know how long ~ : 얼마나 ~하는지 알고 싶습니다.
· connecting flight : 연결 비행편
· that' s about three hours in transit : 환승하는데 약 3시간 걸립니다.
· worry about : 걱정하다(= be worried about).

6. 분실물 문의

SCENE 1

Officer : So, one bag. Is it a suitcase?

Elizabeth : Yes, a green one. It contains documents I need for a meeting today.

Officer : Well, the flight goes on to Rome. I' ll let our office know right away. That' s the best I can do.

Elizabeth : All right. I' m staying at the Novotel. Could you please contact me there?

Key Phrase

- suitcase : 여행용가방
- contain : 포함하다.
- document : 자료, 서류
- let our office know : 사무실에 알려주다.
- contact : 연락을 취하다, 접촉하다.

SCENE 2

Officer : So, one bag. Is it a suitcase?

Elizabeth : No, it' s like a duffel bag.

Officer : When did you last see it?

Elizabeth : I left it under my seat while I went to the bathroom.

Officer : Oh, I' m sorry. Sounds like it' s been stolen. You' ll have to fill in this form for me.

Key Phrase

- duffel bag : 더블 백
- last : ① 마지막 ② 지난번 ③ 지속되다.
- leave-left-left : ① 두다 ② 떠나다.
- (It) sounds like ~ : ~처럼 들리다.
- steal-stole-stolen : 훔치다.
- fill in this form : 이 양식을 작성하다.

SCENE 3

Officer	:	So, one bag. Is it a suitcase?
Elizabeth	:	Yes, a brand new one. It' s very expensive.
Officer	:	Are you insured?
Elizabeth	:	No, unfortunately, I' m not.
Officer	:	Well, we' ll do our best to get it back, ma' am.

Key Phrase

· officer : 직원, 승무원, 공무원, 경찰
· brand new : 신제품
· Are you insured? : 보험에 들었습니까?
· unfortunately : 불운하게도
· do one' s best : 최선을 다하다.
· get it back : 되찾다.

SCENE 4

Officer	:	So, one bag. Is it a suitcase?
Elizabeth	:	No, it' s my purse. Everything I need is in it.
Officer	:	Can you describe it, please?
Elizabeth	:	It' s a brown leather bag with a shoulder strap.
Officer	:	I' ll just have a look at what' s been handed in.

Key Phrase

· purse : 지갑
· Everything I need : 필요한 모든 것
· describe : 설명하다, 묘사하다.
· leather : 가죽
· strap : (가죽) 끈
· what' s been handed in : 접수된 것
cf) hand : 제출하다.

[Situation] Elizabeth is speaking with an officer at the Lost-and-Found.

Elizabeth : I' ve just arrived from Noumea, but my luggage doesn' t seem to be here.

Officer : What flight were you on?

Elizabeth : Air Noumea flight 104.

Officer : Right, that' s Carousel 5, isn' t it?

Elizabeth : Yes, I waited there for half an hour. All the other passengers picked up their bags, but mine wasn' t there.

Officer : One lost bag. Is it a suitcase?

Elizabeth : Yes, a green one.

Officer : I have some pictures here of different kinds of bags. Could you pick out the one that looks most like yours?

Elizabeth : Yes, it looks like number four, but in a soft material.

Officer : OK, could I ask you now to fill in this form? We' ll do what we can to find your bag. Tell me which hotel you' re staying at and we' ll call you there as soon as we have some information.

Elizabeth : OK, thanks.

Key Phrase

- luggage ; 수화물(짐)
- What flight were you on? : 어떤 비행기를 타셨나요?
- for half an hour : 30분 동안
- passengers : 승객
- pick up : 집어가다.
- lose-lost-lost : 분실하다.
- pick out : 고르다(= choose)
- look like ~ : ~처럼 보이다.
- material : 재질
- do what we can : 최선을 다하다.

7. 객실 예약 및 취소

SCENE 1

Elizabeth : I' d like to reserve a room for five nights from the eleventh of next month.

Receptionist : I' m sorry, ma' am, we' re fully booked for next month.

Elizabeth : Oh, that' s disappointing. Well, thank you anyway.

Receptionist : I' m sorry we couldn' t help you. Goodbye.

Key Phrase

· receptionist : 접수원
· I' d like to reserve a room : 방을 예약하고 싶습니다.
· the eleventh of next month : 다음 달 11일
· we' re fully booked : 예약 다 되었습니다.
· disappointing : 실망스러운

SCENE 2

Elizabeth : I' d like to reserve a room for five nights from the eleventh of next month.

Receptionist : Yes, no problem.

Elizabeth : I forgot to ask. There' s a fitness center, isn' t there?

Receptionist : Oh, I' m sorry, ma' am, we don' t actually have one here, but there' s one just around the corner.

Elizabeth : OK then, thank you.

Key Phrase

· forget to ~ : ~하는 것을 잊어버렸습니다.
· fitness center : 헬스클럽
· just around the corner : 바로 모퉁이 근처에

SCENE 3

Elizabeth : I’ d like to reserve a room for five nights from the eleventh of next month.

Receptionist : Sure, ma’ am. Will you be coming by car?

Elizabeth : Yes, I will. Are there parking facilities?

Receptionist : Yes, we have valet parking for an additional daily charge.

Elizabeth : What about a place to park the car without using the valet service?

Receptionist : I’ m sorry, that’ s not possible, ma’ am.

Key Phrase

· parking facilities : 주차시설
· valet parking : 주차 심부름꾼
· additional charge : 추가 비용
· What about ~? : ~을 어떻게 생각하십니까?

SCENE 4

Elizabeth : I’ d like to reserve a room for five nights from the eleventh of next month.

Receptionist : Yes, how many is it for?

Elizabeth : One adult and a child. Do you have day care at the hotel?

Receptionist : Oh, no, we don’ t but we could arrange it for you.

Key Phrase

· how many is it for? : 몇 명이십니까?
  = how many are there in your party?
· daycare center : 보육 시설
· arrange : 준비하다, 예약하다.

[Situation] Elizabeth is telephoning a hotel to make a reservation.

Receptionist : Good morning, Panorama Hotel.

Elizabeth : Oh, good morning. I' m going on vacation next month and I' m trying to find a hotel. Can you tell me about your facilities?

Receptionist : Certainly, ma' am. We' re a four-star hotel just opposite the beach. We have a swimming pool and tennis courts. And there' s a choice of three restaurants.

Elizabeth : That sounds great. What about a TV and VCR?

Receptionist : Yes, there' s a TV in every room, ma' am. We also have an in-house movie selection at no extra charge.

Elizabeth : OK, I' d like to reserve a room for five nights from the eleventh of next month.

Receptionist : I' ll see what we have. We have a room with a private bath, overlooking the beach. Would that be all right?

Elizabeth : Yes, that sounds fine.

Receptionist : I' ll need your name and credit card details as a deposit, please.

Key Phrase

· go on vacation : 휴가를 가다.
· opposite the beach ; 해변 반대편에
· there' s a choice of ~ : ~중에 선택하면 됩니다.
· in-house movie selection : 실내 영화 선택
· at no extra charge : 추가 비용없이
· private bath : 개인 욕실 (↔ public bath 공동 욕실)
· overlooking the beach : 해변이 내려다보이는
· Would that be all right? : 그거면 되겠습니까?
· credit card details : 신용카드 세부항목
· as a deposit : 보증(예약증거)으로서

8. 투숙 절차

SCENE 1

Elizabeth : Could you please reserve a table for six for tonight at the restaurant?

Receptionist : I' m afraid the restaurant is closed for renovations.

Elizabeth : Oh, that' s a shame. We were hoping to have a quick meal.

Receptionist : There are some excellent restaurants in this area, ma' am, not far from here.

Elizabeth : Oh, OK, thanks.

Key Phrase

· a table for six : 6인 식탁
· I' m afraid ~ : 미안하지만 ~
· renovation : 수리
· that' s a shame : 저런

SCENE 2

Receptionist : Can I help you, ma' am?

Elizabeth : Yes, I hope so, I' ve just checked in, but I can' t manage to open my door with this key card. Don' t you have any real keys?

Receptionist : I' m sorry, we only have the key cards now. They work well once you' re used to them. Put it in, wait for the green light and then turn the knob to the right.

Elizabeth : OK, I see. I think I may have tried to turn before the light came on. I' ll try it again, thank you.

Receptionist : My pleasure.

Key Phrase

· manage to ~ : 그럭저럭 ~하다.
· work : 작동하다.
· once you' re used to them : 그것에 익숙하다면
· may have p.p.~ : ~했음에 틀림없군요.

SCENE 3

Receptionist : How will you be paying for your account, Miss Roberts?

Elizabeth : With Diners Club.

Receptionist : Oh, I' m very sorry, ma' am, the hotel does not accept Diners Club.

Elizabeth : Oh, I forgot to ask when I made the reservation.

Receptionist : There' s a bank just opposite the hotel that might be able to help you.

Elizabeth : OK, thanks very much.

Key Phrase

- account : 계산, 계좌
- make the reservation : 예약하다.
- might be able to ~ : ~할 수 있을지도 모릅니다.

SCENE 4

Receptionist : Can I help you, ma' am?

Elizabeth : Yes, thank you. My name' s Elizabeth Roberts. I have a reservation for three nights.

Receptionist : Yes, Miss Roberts. Three nights. You' ll be in room 513 – that' s on the fifth floor.

Elizabeth : There must be a mistake. I reserved a room on the ground floor.

Receptionist : No problem at all. We' ll change your room to a ground floor one immediately.

Elizabeth : Thank you very much.

Key Phrase

- on the fifth floor : 5층에
- the ground floor : 1층
- change ~ to … : ~을 …로 바꾸다.
- immediately : 즉시

[Situation] Elizabeth is checking in to a hotel.

Receptionist : May I help you?

Elizabeth : I have a reservation. My name' s Elizabeth Roberts.

Receptionist : Yes, a single room for three nights with an ocean view. You' ll be in room 506–that' s on the fifth floor. How will you be paying for your account?

Elizabeth : I' ll be paying with Mastercard.

Receptionist : Fine.

Elizabeth : Can you tell me something about the facilities?

Receptionist : This leaflet will help you. It has a map of the city and the hotel. The fax and e–mail facilities are on the third floor.

Elizabeth : Thank you.

Receptionist : Will you be dining here tonight?

Elizabeth : No, I' ll be meeting some friends in the city.

Receptionist : Here is your key card. The bellboy will bring up your luggage. Enjoy your stay.

Elizabeth : Thank you.

Key Phrase

· single room : 일인용 방
· with an ocean view : 바다가 보이는
· facilities : 시설물
· leaflet : 안내지
· bring up : 가지고 올라가다.
· Enjoy your stay : 즐겁게 보내십시오.

9. 객실 시설물 설명

SCENE 1

Bellboy : Here' s your room, Miss Roberts. Enjoy your stay.

Elizabeth : Thank you. What should I do about laundry?

Bellboy : We have a valet laundry service. There are also coin-operated machines on the seventh floor and an iron and an ironing board are in the closet.

Elizabeth : Thanks very much.

Key Phrase

- bellboy : 벨보이, 사환(= bellhop)
- What should I do ~? : 어떻게 할까요?
- laundry : 세탁소
- valet : (호텔의) 보이
- coin-operated machines : 동전투입 세탁기
- closet : 벽장

SCENE 2

Bellboy : Here' s your room, Miss Roberts. Enjoy your stay.

Elizabeth : Thank you. What should I do about getting a crib for my baby?

Bellboy : Did you include it in your reservation?

Elizabeth : Yes, I did.

Bellboy : Just call Housekeeping and they' ll organize it for you.

Key Phrase

- crib : 어린이 침대
- include : 포함하다.
- Housekeeping : 호텔 방 (청소 등의) 관리
- organize : 정리하다.

SCENE 3

Bellboy : Here's your room, Miss Roberts. Enjoy your stay.

Elizabeth : Thank you. I notice there are no tea and coffee facilities.

Bellboy : No problem, ma'am. I'll have Housekeeping organize it for you.

Elizabeth : That'd be great, thank you.

Key Phrase

- notice : 알아채다.
- facilities : 시설물
- I'll have ~ : ~하도록 시키겠습니다.
- That'd be great : 그러면 좋겠습니다.

SCENE 4

Bellboy : Here's your room, Miss Roberts. Enjoy your stay.

Elizabeth : Thank you. I was told I could get a foldaway bed for the room.

Bellboy : No problem, ma'am. Just call Housekeeping and they'll organize it for you.

Elizabeth : Thank you very much.

Key Phrase

- I was told ~ : ~라고 들었습니다.
- get : 구하다.
- a foldaway bed : 접는 침대
- organize : 정리하다.

[Situation] A bellboy shows Elizabeth into a hotel room.

Bellboy : Here you are, ma’ am. This is your room.

Elizabeth : Fine. Put the bags there, please.

Bellboy : I’ ll just open the curtains for you.

Elizabeth : It’ s very cold in here. How do you turn the air conditioning down?

Bellboy : You turn the switch clockwise to make the room warmer.

Elizabeth : OK. What about the television?

Bellboy : Here’ s the remote control. We have local channels and cable TV. If you want to see a video, you select one from the hotel video channel–that’ s channel five.

Elizabeth : And where’ s the fridge?

Bellboy : It’ s right here. There’ s a mini bar and the bottle opener is on the in–side of the fridge door. If you want Room Service, you press seven on the phone.

Wendy : Thanks a lot.

Key Phrase

· turn down : 낮추다.
· air conditioning : 에어컨
· clockwise : 시계방향으로
· What about ~? : ~을 어떻게 생각하십니까?
· remote control : 리모콘
· local channel : 지역방송 채널
· fridge : 냉장고(= refrigerator)
· right here : 바로 여기
· mini bar : 미니 바
· press : 누르다.

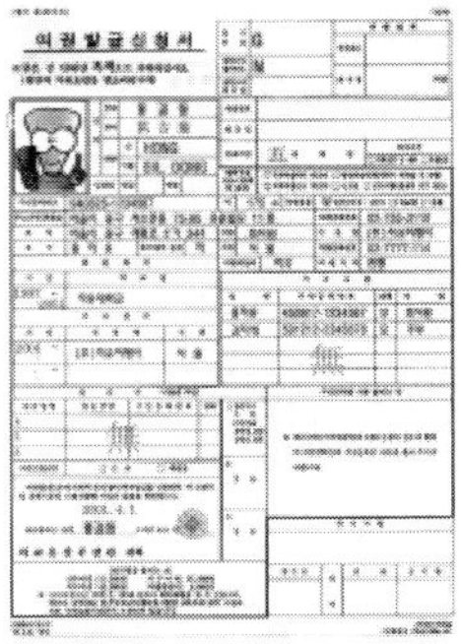

10. 불평 및 문제점 처리

SCENE 1

Receptionist : Hello. Reception. May I help you?

Elizabeth : Yes, I hope so, I' ve just come back to my room after a game of tennis and I' ve discovered that my jewelry box is missing.

Receptionist : Oh, was it in the room safe?

Elizabeth : No, just a drawer in the room.

Receptionist : Could I suggest that you come to Reception and fill out a report and we' ll investigate the matter immediately.

Elizabeth : Yes, I will. Thank you.

Key Phrase

· jewelry box is missing : 보석 상자가 분실되었습니다.
· drawer : 서랍
· investigate the matter : 그 문제를 조사하다.

SCENE 2

Receptionist : Hello. Reception. May I help you?

Elizabeth : Yes, I hope so, Is the manager available?

Receptionist : He' s with someone at the moment. Could I take a message and get him to call you back?

Elizabeth : OK. It' s about my car. I' ve just had my car brought up by the valet and it' s got a nasty scratch along one door.

Receptionist : Oh, I' m very sorry, ma' am. I' ll make sure the Manager calls you as soon as he can.

Elizabeth : Thank you very much.

Key Phrase

· Is the manager available? : 지배인을 만나볼 수 있을까요?

· Could I take your message? : 전하실 말씀이라도 있습니까?
· it' s got a nasty scratch : 그것은 심하게 긁혔습니다.
· I' ll make sure ~ : 반드시 ~하도록 하겠습니다.

SCENE 3

Receptionist	:	Hello. Reception. May I help you?
Elizabeth	:	Yes, I hope so. I want to order dinner from Room Service, but I can' t find the menu in the room.
Receptionist	:	Have you looked in the desk drawer?
Elizabeth	:	No, is it kept there?
Receptionist	:	Usually. Check and see if it' s there and if not, I' ll have another one sent up to you.

Key Phrase

· reception : 접수부
· room service : 룸서비스
· order : 주문하다.
· Is it kept there? : 그곳에 (보관하고) 있습니까?
· see if ~ : ~인지 어떤지 알아보다.
· I' ll have another one sent up : 다른 것을 올려 보내겠습니다.

SCENE 4

Receptionist	:	Hello. Reception. May I help you?
Elizabeth	:	Yes, I hope so. I can' t find my room key.
Receptionist	:	Oh, what room are you in?
Elizabeth	:	Room 707.
Receptionist	:	That' s all right. Just come to Reception and I' ll give you another one.
Elizabeth	:	Thank you very much.

Key Phrase

· what room are you in? 몇 호에 있습니까?
· That' s all right : 괜찮습니다.
· another one : 다른 것

[Situation] Elizabeth is calling Reception from her room.

Receptionist : Good evening. Reception. Mario speaking. What can I do for you?

Elizabeth : Good evening. My name is Elizabeth Roberts. I' m in room 310. I' ve just checked in.

Receptionist : Yes, Miss Roberts.

Elizabeth : There' s a problem with the air conditioning. I can' t turn it down and it' s freezing in here.

Receptionist : I' m sorry, I' ll have it checked for you right away.

Elizabeth : That' s not all. The bathroom hasn' t been cleaned.

Receptionist : I' m so sorry, it should have been cleaned by now. I' ll call Maintenance and have it cleaned for you right away.

Elizabeth : Also, can you do something about the television? There' s a picture but no sound.

Receptionist : Sure, I' ll call Maintenance and have it fixed or replaced immediately. I am very sorry about this, ma' am. I' ll see to these matters right now.

Key Phrase

· (This is) Marie speaking : (전화) 마리입니다.
· What can I do for you? : 무엇을 도와드릴까요?
· I' ve just checked in : 막 투숙했습니다.
· freezing : 몹시 추운
· I' ll have it checked : 점검하도록 시키겠습니다.
· it should have been cleaned by now : 지금쯤 청소되어야 했는데
· Maintenance : 유지보수반
· have it fixed or replaced : 수리하거나 교체하겠습니다.
· see to : 처리하다(= take care of).

11. 정보안내실 찾기

SCENE 1

Attendant : How can I help you?

Elizabeth : Oh, this fax machine seems to be out of paper.

Attendant : Yes, it looks like it is. Let me fill it up for you.

Elizabeth : Thank you very much.

Key Phrase

· attendant : 안내원
· How can I help you? : 도와드릴까요?
· be out of paper : 종이가 부족하다.
· it looks like it is (out of paper) : 종이가 부족한 것 같군요.
· Let me ~ : 제가 ~하겠습니다.
· fill up : 채워 넣다.

SCENE 2

Attendant : How can I help you?

Elizabeth : I' ve been waiting for an urgent fax. I was wondering if it had arrived yet.

Attendant : Well, have you checked with Reception?

Elizabeth : No, not yet. I' ll try there, thank you.

Key Phrase

· urgent fax : 긴급한 팩스
· wonder if ~ : ~인지 어떤지 궁금하다.
· check : 점검하다.
· I' ll try there : 제가 그곳에서 알아보겠습니다.
cf) I' ll try it on : (시험삼아) 입어보겠습니다.

SCENE 3

Attendant : How can I help you?

Elizabeth : Oh, the fax I' ve just received is very faint.

Attendant : Yes, it is. The machine needs more toner. I' ll refill it right away. I suggest that you have the fax sent again.

Elizabeth : Yes, I will, thank you.

Key Phrase

- the fax (that) I' ve just received : 막 도착한 팩스
- faint : (형)희미한, (동)졸도하다.
- toner : 토너(현상액)
- refill : 보충하다
- I suggest that ~ : ~을 제안하다.

SCENE 4

Attendant : How can I help you?

Elizabeth : I' ve been trying to send an e-mail, but I can' t seem to get connected.

Attendant : I' m sorry, there' s been trouble all morning with getting online.

Elizabeth : Should I try again later today?

Attendant : Yes, why don' t you call the center later on and ask if the online connection is working?

Elizabeth : OK, I' ll do that.

Key Phrase

- get connected : 연결하다.
- trouble : 문제, 어려움, 고통
- with getting online : 온라인하는데
- why don' t you ~? : ~하시지 그래요.
- ask if ~ : ~인지 어떤지 물어보다.

[Situation] Elizabeth is talking to the hotel receptionist about the Business Center.

Elizabeth : I' m a guest here in room 506.

Receptionist : Yes, ma' am, how can I help you?

Elizabeth : Could you please tell me how I can send a fax and make some photo-copies?

Receptionist : Certainly, ma' am. You can either leave it with Reception and we' ll organize that for you or you can do it yourself here.

Elizabeth : How do I pay for it?

Receptionist : You can either pay directly at the center or charge it to your account.

Elizabeth : What about e-mail?

Receptionist : The Business Center can help you with that, too. If a fax arrives for you, Reception will bring it up to your room.

Elizabeth : Thank you very much.

Key Phrase

- Could you tell me ~? : ~을 말씀해주시겠습니까?
- send a fax : 팩스를 보내다.
- make a photocopy : 사진복사를 하다.
- either ~ or … : ~이거나 혹은 …이거나
- How do I pay for it? : 어떻게 지불하면 됩니까?
- charge it to your account : 계좌로 청구하다.

12. 방향 안내

SCENE 1

Doorman : Excuse me, ma' am, there' s been some reports recently about bag snatchers in the city. May I suggest you keep a firm hold of your purse today?

Elizabeth : That' s terrible. Thank you for the warning.

Doorman : That' s OK. Better to be safe than sorry.

Elizabeth : Yes, that' s right.

Key Phrase

· doorman : 현관안내원
· bag snatcher : 날치기
· keep hold of : 간직하다
· firm : 확고한, 단단한
· That' s terrible : 무서운 일이군요.
· warning : 경고
· (it is) Better to be safe than sorry : 후회하는 것보다 안전한 것이 낫다.

SCENE 2

Elizabeth : Could you help me with this map, please?

Doorman : Certainly, ma' am.

Elizabeth : I can' t find Riley Street.

Doorman : Riley Street is not easy to find. Let me show you where it is.

Key Phrase

· help ~ with … : ~에게 …을 도와주다.
· easy to find : 찾기 쉽다.
· Let me show you where it is : 어디인지 안내해 드리겠습니다.

SCENE 3

Elizabeth : I need to be at the airport in 45 minutes. How long does the shuttle bus take to get there?

Doorman : At this time of day, it takes around an hour.

Elizabeth : Would a taxi be faster?

Doorman : Yes, it would.

Key Phrase

- be at the airport : 공항에 도착하다.
- in 45 minutes : 45분 후에
- How long does ~ take to get there? : ~가 그곳에 가는데 얼마나 걸립니까?
- At this time of day : 오늘 이맘 때

SCENE 4

Elizabeth : Can you recommend somewhere quick to get a snack before the theater?

Doorman : There' s a little Italian restaurant down the end of this street. It' s very good.

Elizabeth : I tried there last night, but it was very crowded.

Doorman : It' s still quite early. It probably isn' t crowed right now.

Elizabeth : OK, thanks very much.

Key Phrase

- recommend : 추천하다.
- get a snack : 간단한 식사
- try : (맛보려고) 시도하다.
- crowded : 붐비다.
- probably : 아마도

[Situation] Elizabeth walks up to the doorman of her hotel.

Doorman : Yes, ma' am?

Elizabeth : I need some directions. I' d like to do some shopping at one of the big department stores.

Doorman : Most of the big stores are downtown, around Central Square.

Elizabeth : What' s the best way to get there?

Doorman : If you go by bus, it takes about 20 minutes. There' s a bus station a block away from here on this side of the road.

Elizabeth : What about going by train?

Doorman : The subway takes less time and the subway station isn' t far from here. You go out of the hotel, turn right and it' s a five-minute walk.

Elizabeth : OK, thanks a lot. Also, I' ll be needing a taxi to the airport this after-noon. Can you order one for me?

Doorman : Yes, ma' am. What time do you need to be at the airport?

Elizabeth : Five o' clock.

Doorman : There' s a lot of traffic at that time. So it' ll take around an hour. I' ll ask the taxi to be here at four.

Elizabeth : OK, fine. I' ll be ready then. Thanks very much.

Doorman : You' re very welcome, ma' am.

Key Phrase

· direction : 방향, 지시
· Most of ~ : 대부분의 ~
· take less time : 시간이 덜 걸리다.
· a five-minute walk : 걸어서 5분 걸리는 거리
· a lot of traffic : 많은 교통량

13. 퇴숙 및 요금 지불

SCENE 1

Receptionist : Could I have your room number, please?
Elizabeth : Yes, room 201.
Receptionist : I' m sorry, could you repeat that, please?
Elizabeth : Sure, I' m in room 201.
Receptionist : And you stayed for two nights?
Elizabeth : Yes.

Key Phrase

· check out : 퇴숙하다.
· pay the account : 요금을 지불하다.
· Could you have your room number? : 방번호를 알려주십시오.
· Could you repeat that? : 다시 말씀해주시겠습니까?

SCENE 2

Receptionist : Thank you. I' ll get your bill... Here you are, Miss Roberts.
Elizabeth : I think there' s been a mistake. I didn' t make any phone calls.
Receptionist : Oh, I' ll just check your details... I' m very sorry, ma' am, there has been a mistake. I' ll deduct ten dollars from your bill.
Elizabeth : Thank you.
Receptionist : I do apologize. How would you like to pay?

Key Phrase

· I' ll get your bill : 계산서를 가져오겠습니다.
· make a phone call : 전화를 걸다.
· details : 세부내용
· deduct : 공제하다.
· apologize : 사과하다.

SCENE 3

Receptionist : Thank you. I' ll get your bill... Here you are, Miss Roberts. How would you like to pay?

Elizabeth : By credit card. Do you take Visa?

Receptionist : Certainly, ma' am... I' m sorry, your card has expired. Do you have another one?

Elizabeth : Oh, I' m sorry. Do you take Diners Club?

Receptionist : Certainly, ma' am... Could you sign here, please? That' s fine... Here' s your receipt.

Key Phrase

· I' ll get your bill : 계산서를 가져오겠습니다.
· Here you are : 여기 있습니다.
· How would you like to pay? : 어떻게 지불하겠습니까?
· your card has expired : 카드가 기한이 지났군요.
· another one : 다른 것
· receipt : 영수증

SCENE 4

Receptionist : Thank you. I' ll get your bill... Here you are, Miss Roberts. How would you like to pay?

Elizabeth : Do you take Mastercard?

Receptionist : I' m sorry, we don' t, ma' am. Do you have another one?

Elizabeth : Visa?

Receptionist : Certainly, ma' am. Thank you... Could you sign here, please? That' s fine... Here' s your receipt.

Key Phrase

· Certainly : 좋습니다.
· Could you sign here? : 사인해주시겠습니까?

[Situation] Elizabeth is checking out of a hotel.

Elizabeth	:	I' d like to check out now.
Receptionist	:	Certainly ma' am. could I have your name, please?
Elizabeth	:	Yes, it' s Elizabeth Roberts.
Receptionist	:	Could you spell your last name, please?
Elizabeth	:	Sure. It' s R-O-B-E-R-T-S.
Receptionist	:	Could you tell me your room number, please?
Elizabeth	:	Yes, room 201.
Receptionist	:	And you stayed for two nights?
Elizabeth	:	Yes, I did.
Receptionist	:	Thank you. I' ll get your bill... Here you are, Miss Roberts. How would you like to pay?
Elizabeth	:	By credit card. do you take Visa?
Receptionist	:	Certainly, ma' am. Thank you.... Could you sign here, please? That' s fine... Here' s your receipt.
Elizabeth	:	Thank you.
Receptionist	:	I hope you' ve enjoyed your stay.
Elizabeth	:	Yes, very much.
Receptionist	:	Goodbye, ma' am.
Elizabeth	:	Goodbye.

Key Phrase

· Could I have your name? : 이름을 말씀해주십시오.
· Could you spell ~? : ~의 철자를 말씀해주십시오.
· I hope you' ve enjoyed your stay : 즐거운 시간을 보내십시오.

14. 접대 및 착석

SCENE 1

Elizabeth : I wonder if you' d mind checking the total of this bill.

Waiter : Is there a problem?

Elizabeth : Yes, I think there might be a mistake.

Waiter : Certainly, ma' am, just a moment.

Key Phrase

- I wonder if ~ : ~인지 어떤지 궁금합니다.
- mind ~ing : ~을 꺼려하다.
- the total of this bill : 청구서 합계
- there might be a mistake : 실수가 있을지도 모른다.

SCENE 2

Waiter : What was the name on the reservation?

Elizabeth : Roberts.

Waiter : What time was the reservation for?

Elizabeth : It was for 12 o' clock.

Waiter : I' m sorry, there doesn' t seem to be any record of it in the reservation book.

Key Phrase

- the name on the reservation : 예약상의 이름
- What time was the reservation for? : 예약 시간은 언제입니까?
- reservation book : 예약부

SCENE 3

Elizabeth : I think I must have been put in the smoking section. There are people smoking over there.

Waiter : Yes, ma' am, this is the smoking section.

Elizabeth : Well, I asked to be put in non-smoking.

Waiter : I' m very sorry, ma' am. Would you like to move?

Key Phrase

- must have p.p. ~ : ~했음에 틀림없다.
- be put in ~ : ~에 들어가다.
- smoking section : 흡연 구역
- non-smoking section : 비흡연 구역
- Would you like to move? : 자리를 옮기시겠습니까?

SCENE 4

Waiter : Are you ready to order, ma' am?

Elizabeth : Well, I' d... I' d like to, but I' m a vegetarian and I can' t find anything on the menu to eat.

Waiter : You' ll find all the vegetarian dishes on the back page.

Elizabeth : Oh, OK, thank you. Can you come back in a few minutes and I' ll order then?

Waiter : Of course, ma' am.

Key Phrase

- Are you ready to order? : 주문하시겠습니까?
- vegetarian : 채식주의자
- dishes : 요리, 음식
  cf) side dish : 반찬, 안주

[Situation] A waiter welcomes Elizabeth to the restaurant at the hotel.

Waiter : Good afternoon, ma' am. Do you have a reservation?

Elizabeth : Yes, in the name of Roberts. I' m staying at the hotel.

Waiter : Yes, here we are. A table for one at twelve o' clock. Let me take your coat. Now, there' s a table near the window or one out on the terrace. Which one would you prefer?

Elizabeth : It' s a bit cold today. I think I' ll stay inside.

Waiter : Very well. Let me show you to your table... Here is the menu. Let me tell you about our specials today. The fish of the day is snapper and the soup is chicken noodle. Would you like a drink before ordering?

Elizabeth : Yes, I' ll have a light beer.

Waiter : Certainly, ma' am. I' ll be back to take your order.

Key Phrase

- Do you have a reservation? : 예약하셨습니까?
- in the name of ~ : ~라는 이름으로
- Let me take your coat : 코트를 받아주겠습니다.
- terrace : 테라스
- Which one would you prefer? : 어떤 것을 더 좋아하십니까?
- Let me show you to ~ : ~로 안내해드리겠습니다.
- specials : 특별 요리
- snapper : 도미(의 일종)
- I' ll be back : 돌아오겠습니다.

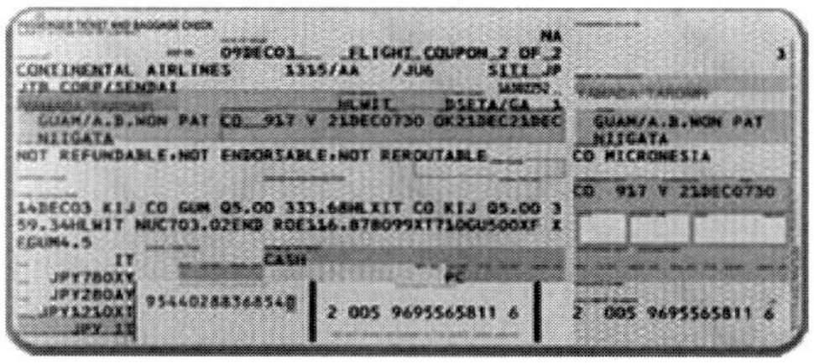

15. 음료수 주문

SCENE 1

Elizabeth : Excuse me, Bartender!

Bartender : Yes, ma' am. Do you want to order a drink?

Elizabeth : Yes, I' ve changed my mind. I do want a drink. Can you bring me a gin and tonic, please?

Bartender : Certainly, ma' am.

Key Phrase

· Bartender : 바텐더
· Do you want to order a drink? : 마실 것을 주문하시겠습니까?
· a gin and tonic : 진 토닉(진과 토닉 워터)

SCENE 2

Elizabeth : Excuse me, Bartender!

Bartender : Yes, ma' am. Is there a problem?

Elizabeth : This beer is not what I expected. Is it imported or local?

Bartender : It' s a local brand, ma' am.

Elizabeth : Oh, well, I ordered an imported beer. Would you mind changing it, please?

Bartender : Yes, ma' am, no problem at all.

Key Phrase

· ~ What I expected : 내가 기대한 것
· imported or local : 수입된 것인지 국산품인지
· local brand : 국산품
· Would you mind changing it? : 바꿔주시겠습니까?

SCENE 3

Bartender : Here you are, ma'am, one white wine.

Elizabeth : White wine? I'm sorry, but I ordered a red wine.

Bartender : Did you? I'm very sorry. I'll take this back and get you a red one.

Elizabeth : Thank you very much.

Key Phrase

- take back : 도로 가져가다.
- get you a red one : 빨간 것으로 가져다 드리겠습니다.

SCENE 4

Elizabeth : Excuse me, Bartender!

Bartender : Yes, ma'am, is there something wrong?

Elizabeth : Yes, this club soda is very flat. Could you bring me another one, please?

Bartender : Yes, I'm very sorry about that, ma'am.

Key Phrase

- (is there) something wrong? : 잘못된 것이 있습니까?
- club soda : 클럽 소다(소다수 이름)
- flat : 김빠진, 단조로운, 평평한
- Could you bring me another one? : 다른 것 가져다 주실래요?

탄산음료(Carbonated Drink, Sparkling Drink)**의 종류**

① 소다수(Soda Water) : 플레인 소오다(Plain Soda), 에리이터 워터(Aerated Water), 클럽소다(Club Soda) ② 토닉워터(Tonic Water) ③ 카린스 믹서(Collins Mixer) ④ 진저엘(Ginger Ale) ⑤ 콜라(Cola) ⑥ 사이다(Cider, Cidre) ⑦ 세븐업(7Up), 스프라이트(Sprite) ⑧ 진저비어(Ginger Beer) ⑨ 과라나(Guarana)

[Situation] Elizabeth and a friend are sitting at the bar in a hotel.

Bartender : What can I get you?
Elizabeth : I' ll have a glass of wine, please.
Bartender : Sure. Red or white?
Elizabeth : White, please. I' d like a very dry wine.
Bartender : I' m sorry, we don' t have any very dry whites, but we do have a nice medium-dry one.
Elizabeth : Oh, OK, I' ll have a beer instead. Do you have any imported beer?
Bartender : No, I' m sorry, we don' t have any imported beer. But we do have some very good local beers.
Elizabeth : All rights. That' ll be fine.
Bartender : Will that be all?
Elizabeth : Do you have any snacks?
Bartender : Sure. We have nuts, corn chips and pretzels.
Elizabeth : Could I have some corn chips, please?
Bartender : No problem, ma' am.

Key Phrase

· What can I get you? : 무엇을 가져다 드릴까요?
· dry wine : 톡 쏘는(달콤한 종류가 아닌) 포도주(↔ sweet wine)
· medium-dry one : 중간 맛의 포도주
· Will that be all? : 그게 전부입니까?
· snacks : 간식, 가벼운 식사
· nuts : 밤
· peanuts : 땅콩
· corn chips : 콘
· pretzels : 프레츨(안주용 비스켓의 일종)

16. 음식 주문

SCENE 1

Waiter : Are you ready to order your first course?
Elizabeth : I' ll have the fish of the day, please.
Waiter : I' m very sorry, there' s none left.
Elizabeth : Oh, what can you recommend then?

Key Phrase

· Are you ready to order ~? : ~을 주문하시겠습니까?
· first course : 첫 번째 코스
· the fish of the day : 오늘의 어류요리
cf) the play of the day : 오늘의 최고 멋진 경기
· there' s none left : 남은 게 없습니다.
· recommend : 추천하다.

SCENE 2

Waiter : Can I take your order, please?
Elizabeth : Sure. Can we get some wine with the meal, too
Waiter : I' m very sorry, we don' t have a liquor license.
Elizabeth : Oh, I didn' t know that.

Key Phrase

· Can I take your order? : 주문하시겠습니까?
· meal : 식사
· liquor license : 주류 면허증

SCENE 3

Waiter : Are you ready to order?
Elizabeth : Yes, I'd like to start with the oysters, please.
Waiter : I'm sorry, there's none left. They've been very popular today.
Elizabeth : Oh, that's disappointing. I really felt like having oysters.

Key Phrase

· oysters : 굴
· popular : 인기있는
· disappointing : 실망스러운
· feel like ~ing : ~을 하고 싶다.
· I really felt like having oysters.
  = I' d really like to have oysters.

SCENE 4

Waiter : Here you are. One soup and one salad.
Elizabeth : I think there' s been some mistake. I didn' t order a salad.
Waiter : Oh, I am sorry. I misunderstood.
Elizabeth : That' s all right.

Key Phrase

· misunderstand : 잘못 이해하다.
· That' s all right : 괜찮습니다.
  cf) That' s right : 맞습니다.

[Situation] Elizabeth is sitting at her restaurant table.

Waiter : Good afternoon, ma' am. Here is your menu and wine list. The soup of the day is minestrone and the fish of the day is ocean trout. I' ll be back to take your order when you' re ready. Would you like a drink before your meal?

Elizabeth : No, thank you.

(A few minutes later, the waiter returns.)

Waiter : Are you ready to order now, ma' am?

Elizabeth : What' s the trout like today?

Waiter : Oh, it' s very nice. It' s pan-fried and served with a herb sauce.

Elizabeth : OK. I' ll have the steak.

Waiter : How would you like that cooked?

Elizabeth : Medium rare, thanks. Oh, what' s that served with?

Waiter : It' s served with vegetables and a mushroom sauce.

Elizabeth : That' s fine.

Waiter : So, that' s one medium-rare steak. would you like a side salad?

Elizabeth : No, thank you. But could I also have a bottle of mineral water please?

Waiter : Certainly, ma' am. The wine waiter will be along in a minute to take your order.

Key Phrase

· wine list : 포도주 목록표
· minestrone : 미네즈트로우니(진한 수프의 일종)
· ocean trout : 바다 송어
· What' s the trout like today? : 오늘 송어는 어떻습니까?
· pan-fried : 후라이팬으로 튀긴
· herb sauce : 허브 소스(cf. herb 약초)
· What' s that served with? : 그것은(그 음식은) 어떻게 제공됩니까?
· will be along : 뒤따를 겁니다.

17. 고충 처리

SCENE 1

Waiter : This is your table.

Elizabeth : Oh, but look, the tablecloth is stained.

Waiter : You' re right. I didn' t notice. I' ll change it for you immediately.

Elizabeth : Thank you.

Key Phrase

· tablecloth : 식탁보
· stained : 얼룩진
· notice : 알아차리다.
· immediately : 즉시(= right now)

SCENE 2

Waiter : Is there anything wrong, ma' am?

Elizabeth : Yes, this glass is chipped.

Waiter : Oh dear, I' m very sorry. I' ll replace it right away.

Elizabeth : Thank you.

Key Phrase

· (Is there) Anything wrong? : 잘못된 것이 있습니까?
· chipped : 금이 간
· replace : 대체하다.
· right away : 당장

SCENE 3

Waiter	:	Is there anything wrong, ma' am?
Elizabeth	:	Yes, actually, this chicken is much too spicy. I ordered it mild.
Waiter	:	I' m sorry, ma' am. I' ll take it back to the kitchen and bring you a mild one.
Elizabeth	:	Thank you very much.

Key Phrase

· actually : 실제로, 사실(= in fact)
· too spicy : 너무 매운
· mild : 부드러운, 온화한
· take back : 도로 가져가다.

SCENE 4

Waiter	:	Is there anything wrong, ma' am?
Elizabeth	:	It' s the white wine, Waiter. It' s at room temperature. It' s supposed to be chilled.
Waiter	:	I' m very sorry, ma' am. I' ll get you a chilled one right away.
Elizabeth	:	Thank you very much.

Key Phrase

· at room temperature : 실내온도에
· It' s supposed to be chilled : 차가워야 하는데요.
cf) be supposed to ~ : ~해야 하는데요.
· I' ll get you a chilled one : 차가운 것을 가져다 드리겠습니다.

[Situation] Elizabeth is in a restaurant. She is complaining to the waiter.

Waiter : Is there anything wrong, ma' am?

Elizabeth : Ah, my steak is too rare. It' s supposed to be medium rare.

Waiter : I' m sorry, ma' am. I' ll take it back to the kitchen and get you another one. And this time I' ll make sure it' s medium rare.

Elizabeth : And my vegetables are too cold. They' re supposed to be warm.

Waiter : I' m very sorry. I' ll speak to the chef and bring you some warm vegetables.

Elizabeth : And another thing. I' ve been waiting for the wine waiter for twenty minutes now.

Waiter : I' ll see to it right away. I' ll send him to your table at once. The problem is we' re short-staffed tonight. Two of our waiters are sick.

Elizabeth : Also, the music' s too loud. Could you turn it down?

Waiter : Yes, of course.

Key Phrase

· too rare : 너무 설익은
· medium rare : 보통으로 익힌
· I' ll make sure ~ : 반드시 ~하겠습니다.
· vegetables : 야채
· chef : 주방장
· Another thing : 하나 더
· I' ll see to it : 제가 처리하겠습니다.
· see to = take care of
· short-staffed 직원이 부족한
· too loud : 너무 시끄러운
· turn down : 낮추다, 거절하다.
ex) Sandra Block turned down Bruce Willis' proposal.

18. 공항에서 손님맞이

SCENE 1

Guide : OK. Are you ready to go?
Elizabeth : Well, no. My luggage hasn' t turned up yet.
Guide : Let' s have another look on the carousel.
Elizabeth : All right. I hope it' s there this time.

Key Phrase

· guide ; 가이드, 안내원
· luggage : 수화물(= baggage)
· turn up : 나타나다(= appear).
· carousel : 회전식 원형 콘베이어
· this time : 이번에는

SCENE 2

Elizabeth : Hello. My name' s Elizabeth Roberts.
Guide : Welcome to Sydney. How was your trip?
Elizabeth : It was fine except I feel very sick. I think I might have caught the flu.
Guide : Well, I suggest we go straight to the hotel and you can see a doctor there if you like.

Key Phrase

· How was your trip? : 여행은 어떠했습니까?
· except ~ : ~을 제외하고
· might have caught the flu : 감기에 걸렸을지도 모른다.
cf) catch – caught – caught
· I suggest ~ : ~을 제안합니다.
· go straight : 바로 가다.

SCENE 3

Elizabeth	: You must be Mr. Atkins?
Guide	: That' s right. And you' re Miss Robertson?
Elizabeth	: No, it' s Miss Roberts.
Guide	: Oh, I' m sorry, my mistake.

Key Phrase

· You must be ~ : 당신 ~임에 틀림없군요.
cf) You must study hard : 열심히 공부해야 합니다.
· must have p.p. ~ : ~했음에 틀림없다.
· You must have studied very hard : 당신은 열심히 공부했음에 틀림없군요.

SCENE 4

Guide	: How was your trip?
Elizabeth	: It was fine, but I didn' t manage to get any sleep.
Guide	: That' s a shame.
Elizabeth	: Yes, I... I' d like to get to the hotel and have a rest.

Key Phrase

· manage to ~ : 가까스로 ~하다.
· get sleep : 잠을 자다.
· That' s a shame
· get to ~ : ~에 도착하다.
· have(take) a rest : 휴식을 취하다.

[Situation] In the arrival hall of Sydney Airport, a man is holding up a sign that says 'Sunshine Tours'. Elizabeth is coming out of Immigration and Customs and walks towards him.

Elizabeth : You must be Mr. Atkins from Sunshine Tours.

Guide : That's right, Freddie Atkins. And you must be Miss Roberts from the United States, is that right?

Elizabeth : Yes, I'm Wendy Roberts.

Guide : Pleased to meet you. Welcome to Sydney. How was your flight? You must be tired.

Elizabeth : A little bit, but I managed to get some sleep.

Guide : Is this your first visit to Australia?

Elizabeth : Oh, actually, I was here for a week last year.

Guide : Well, I hope you have an enjoyable trip. First, we'll go to your hotel, the Boulevard. It's right in the center of town.

Elizabeth : Good. I can drop off my luggage and freshen up before lunch.

Key Phrase

· (I'm) pleased to meet you : 만나서 기뻤습니다.
· How was your flight? : 비행(여행)은 어떠했습니까?
· A little bit : 약간
· right in the center of town : 바로 시내 중앙에
· drop off : 풀다, 내리다.
· freshen up : 바람을 쏘이다.

19. 관광 정보 제공

SCENE 1

Guide : You' re joining the lakes tour tomorrow, aren' t you?

Elizabeth : Yes, that' s right. What time will the bus pick me up?

Guide : The bus will be at your hotel at 5:30 A.M.

Elizabeth : 5:30! I can' t get up that early!

Key Phrase

· lakes tour : 호수 여행
· pick up : 태우러 가다(오다)
· 5:30 : five thirty
· A.M. : ante meridiem(=before noon) ad., a. 오전에(의)
· P.M. : post meridiem(=after midday) ad., a. 오후(의)

SCENE 2

Elizabeth : I' d like to visit the underground tombs.

Guide : Sure, there' s a tour leaving at 3 P.M.

Elizabeth : I' d like to join it. Are you allowed to take pictures?

Guide : No, cameras are forbidden in the tombs.

Key Phrase

· underground tombs : 지하 무덤
· there' s a tour leaving at 3 P.M. : 오후 3시에 출발하는 여행이 있다.
· join it : 참여하다.
· Are you allowed to ~? : ~을 허락합니까?
· take pictures : 사진을 찍다.
· forbidden : 금지된
cf) forbid – forbade – forbidden

SCENE 3

Guide : The tour leaves at 7:30 in the morning.
Elizabeth : Will the bus pick me up at the hotel?
Guide : No, you have to go to Central Station to join the tour.
Elizabeth : I think that' s going to be difficult.

Key Phrase

· pick up : 태우러 오다(가다).
· have to ~ : ~해야 합니다.
· that' s going to be difficult : 그것은 어려울 거라고 생각됩니다.

SCENE 4

Guide : The day tour of the city costs 50 dollars per person.
Elizabeth : Does that include the price of lunch?
Guide : No, I' m sorry it doesn' t. Lunch will be extra.
Elizabeth : It' s very expensive then.

Key Phrase

· day tour : 일일 여행
· cost : 비용이 ~들다.
· include : 포함하다.
· extra : 추가되는

[Situation] A tour guide is in a hotel lobby. He is talking to Elizabeth who requires information about tours of the city.

Elizabeth : I' d like to get some information about day tours of the city.

Guide : Sure, no problem. There are several bus tours you can take that show you the sights.

Elizabeth : Can you get off the bus to take pictures and visit places?

Guide : On most of these tours you can stop, walk around and take pictures.

Elizabeth : What about the itinerary? Do they all go to the same place?

Guide : Roughly. I have some brochures here that' ll give you all the information you need to have about costs and times. The cheapest is the Blue Tours Company. Their tours leave Battery Park at nine o' clock and you buy your own lunch.

Elizabeth : And the other? What do you get if you pay more?

Guide : Big Apple tours cost more than the others, but the price includes a restaurant lunch. They' ll also pick you up at your hotel and take you back there, so it' s a great package deal.

Key Phrase

· require : 요구하다.
· sights : 경치
· get off : 내리다.
· What about ~? : ~을 어떻게 생각하십니까?
· itinerary : 여행일정표
· Roughly : 대충
· brochure : 브로슈어, 소책자
· What do you get? : 어떤 것을 구할 수 있습니까?
· package deal : 패키지 상품

20. 렌트카 정보 제공

SCENE 1

Receptionist : Acme Cars. Mario speaking. Can I help you?

Elizabeth : Look, I' m really sorry. I rented one of your cars this morning and I' ve locked myself out of it.

Receptionist : Just tell me where you are at the moment and we' ll have someone come and unlock the car for you.

Elizabeth : Thank you so much.

Receptionist : I' m sorry, we' ll have to charge you for this.

Elizabeth : Yes, I understand.

Key Phrase

- provide ; 제공하다.
- rental cars : 렌트카, 자동차대여
- (This is) Mary speaking : 메리입니다(전화).
- lock myself out of a car : 차 문이 잠기다.
- unlock : 열다.

SCENE 2

Receptionist : Acme Cars. Mario speaking. Can I help you?

Elizabeth : Yes, I notice here on the account that I' ve been charged for the delivery.

Receptionist : Yes, that' s right.

Elizabeth : I understood that it was free.

Receptionist : I don' t know how you got that information. We always charge a deliv-ery fee.

Key Phrase

- notice : 알아차리다.
- account : 계산서
- charge : 청구하다.
- free (of charge): 무료
- delivery fee : 배달요금

SCENE 3

Receptionist : Acme Cars. Mario speaking. Can I help you?

Elizabeth : Yes, one of your drivers has just delivered a car, but it' s a stickshift. I asked for an automatic. there must be some mistake.

Receptionist : I' m sorry, I' ll fix the problem right away.

Elizabeth : Could you deliver the car within the next hour? I' ve got a business meeting to go to.

Receptionist : Yes, ma' am, that won' t be a problem.

Key Phrase

· stickshift : 수동 변속기
· automatic (shift) : 자동 변속기
· a business meeting to go to : 가야할 사업 모임

SCENE 4

Receptionist : Acme Cars. Mario speaking. Can I help you?

Elizabeth : My name' s Elizabeth Roberts. The car I rented is parked in the hotel garage. I' ve locked it and given the keys to the Concierge.

Receptionist : Thank you, ma' am. We' ll send someone to pick it up.

Elizabeth : There' s just one thing. I' ve had a small accident and there' s a tiny dent in the fender.

Receptionist : I' ll make a note of that. I' m sorry, we' ll have to add a repair charge to your bill.

Elizabeth : I understand. That' s all right, thank you.

Key Phrase

· garage : 차고
· Concierge : (호텔 출입문의) 문지기
· pick up : 가지고 오다, 데리러 오다.
· tiny dent in the fender : 펜더(흙받이)에 작은 (오목한) 흠
· make a not of : 노트에 적다.

[Situation] The hotel receptionist is giving information to Elizabeth about rental car companies.

Receptionist : How can I help you, ma' am?

Elizabeth : I want to rent a car for a week from tomorrow so I can travel around the island. Can you tell me what' s available?

Receptionist : Yes, of course. What kind of car do you want?

Elizabeth : Medium sized. A stickshift, if possible. And it has to be reliable. I don' t want something that' ll break down. A friend of mine had gearbox problems with a rental car last week and lost half a day waiting for a replacement.

Receptionist : Oh, that was unlucky. Well, we have two rental car companies here – Overland Rentals and Acme. Both are very reliable. I' m sure you won' t have any problems with either of them.

Elizabeth : I hope not. How do the prices compare?

Receptionist : A medium-size car costs 48 dollars with Overland Rentals and 56 dollars with Acme, but Acme guarantees immediate replacement anywhere on the island in two hours if the car breaks down. Neither of them will charge you for delivery.

Elizabeth : I think Acme would be a safer choice.

Key Phrase

· what' s available : 이용가능한 것
· what kind of car ~? : 어떤 종류의 차를 ~?
· reliable : 믿을 만한
· break down : 고장나다.
· replacement : 교체, 교체품, 교체자
· guarantee : 보장하다
· Neither of them ~ : 그 둘 다 ~ 아니다.

21. 여행 일정 구성

SCENE 1

Guide : Has anyone forgotten their camera? Does anyone have any idea who it belongs to?

Elizabeth : A few couples got off at the last stop. Maybe it belongs to one of them.

Guide : Yes, you might be right. I' ll contact the Reservations Office and see if I can find out where they' re staying. If you happen to see them, please let them know it' s here.

Elizabeth : Sure.

Key Phrase

- belong to ~ : ~에 속하다.
- contact : 연락을 취하다.
- happen to V ~ : 우연히 ~하다.

SCENE 2

Elizabeth : Oh no, my jacket! I left my jacket on the bus and it' s gone!

Guide : Don' t worry. I' ll phone their office on my cell phone and ask them to hold the jacket at the office until you can pick it up.

Elizabeth : Oh, that' s great. Is the office far from here?

Guide : No, not very far. I can show you how to get there if you like.

Elizabeth : Thank you very much.

Key Phrase

- it' s gone : 그것은(버스는) 가버렸습니다.
- cell phone : 휴대폰 cf) hand phone(×)
- hold ~ at the office : 사무실에 ~을 간직하다.
- ~ how to get there : 그곳에 가는 방법

SCENE 3

Guide	:	OK, is everyone ready? I hope you' ve all remembered to bring a hat and a bottle of water. It will get very hot by the middle of the day.
Elizabeth	:	Oh no, I left my hat and water in the hotel! What should I do?
Guide	:	Well, we always bring a few extras in case this happens.
Elizabeth	:	Thank you. I am so sorry to bother you!
Guide	:	Don' t worry about it. You' ll remember next time.

Key Phrase

· get very hot : 매우 더워지다.
· in case ~ : ~하는 경우에
· I am sorry to bother you : 당신을 귀찮게 해서 죄송합니다.

SCENE 4

Guide	:	I have an announcement to make. Because of bad weather conditions, today' s helicopter flight has been canceled. We will notify everyone when the weather improves.
Elizabeth	:	Unfortunately, today' s my last day here.
Guide	:	Well, if you come with me, ma' am. I' ll refund your ticket for you.
Elizabeth	:	Thanks, that' d be great.

Key Phrase

· make an announcement : 발표하다.
· Because of ~ : ~ 때문에(= Due to, On account of)
· weather conditions : 날씨 조건
· cancel : 취소하다(= call off).
· notify : 통보하다.
· improve : 좋아지다. 개선되다.
· refund : (동)환불하다. (명)환불

[Situation] Elizabeth who has reservations on two tours. She is sitting in the hotel lobby.

Guide : I won' t keep you for long. Now, you have reservations on two different tours. You' re going on the scenic flight and on the bus tour to the tropical rain forest.

Elizabeth : What time does the flight leave?

Guide : The flight departs the Valley Airport on Wednesday at 6 A.M. So the bus will pick everyone up here at 5:30, so everyone going on the scenic flight will have to get up early.

Elizabeth : What do I need to take?

Guide : It will be cold, so take some warm clothes. Don' t forget your camera. You' ll be flying over the volcano and the lakes and returning at noon.

Elizabeth : What about the bus tour? I have reservations on that, too.

Guide : That' s on Tuesday. The bus will be here to pick you up at 8 A.M. Now the forest floor is wet, so we insist that everyone going to the rain forest wear good strong shoes.

Key Phrase

· for long : 오래동안
· scenic flight : 경치가 좋은(멋진) 비행
· tropical rain forest : 열대우림지역
· depart : 출발하다.
· volcano : 화산
· forest floor : 산림지대
· insist : 주장하다, 강조하다.

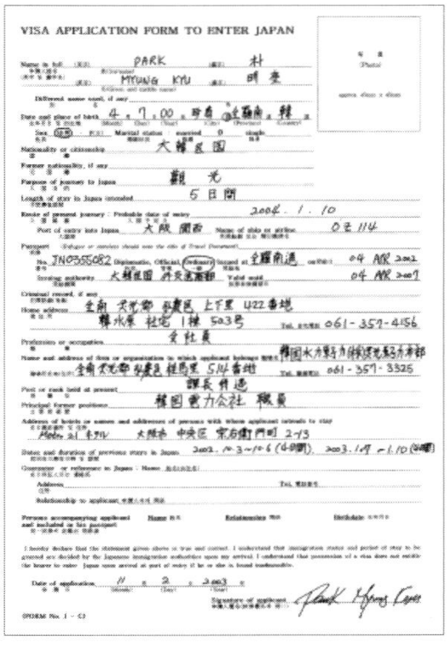
VISA APPLICATION FORM TO ENTER JAPAN

Name in full: PARK 朴
MYUNG KYU 明奎

Date and place of birth: 4. 7. 00.

Nationality or citizenship: 大韓民国

Purpose of journey to Japan: 観光

Length of stay in Japan intended: 5日間

Route of present journey: Probable date of entry: 2004. 1. 10

Port of entry into Japan: 大阪 関西 Name of ship or airline: OZ 114

Passport No. JN0355082 Diplomatic, Official, (Ordinary)

Date of issue: 04 APR 2002 Valid until: 04 APR 2007

Tel. 061-357-4156

Tel. 061-357-3325

Date of application: 11. 2. 2003

FORM No. 1 - C)

22. 분실물 처리

SCENE 1

Elizabeth : Oh, no, my wallet. It' s... it' s gone!

Guide : When did you see it last?

Elizabeth : It must have been when I paid the taxi driver. I put it back in my pocket then.

Guide : Maybe it' s been stolen.

Elizabeth : Yes, maybe I' ve been robbed.

Key Phrase

- wallet : 지갑(cf. purse)
- it' s gone : 사라지다(분실하다).
- last : (부)마지막으로, (동)지속되다.
- must have p.p. ~ : ~했음에 틀림없다.
- Maybe it' s been stolen : 아마도 분실되었을지도 모릅니다.
- maybe I' ve been robbed : 도난당할 수도 있어요.

SCENE 2

Guide : You collected all your luggage?

Elizabeth : One bag has come in, but I' m waiting for the second one.

Guide : It' s surprising that they' re not both together.

Elizabeth : Yes, that' s why I' m worried about the second one.

Key Phrase

- collect : 모으다, 수거하다.
- that' s why ~ : 그것이 ~한 이유입니다.
- be worried about ~ : ~을 걱정하다.

SCENE 3

Guide : Excuse me, Miss.

Elizabeth : Yes?

Guide : Do you know your backpack is open and anyone could be stealing your things?

Elizabeth : No, I... I didn' t realize that. I' ll close it up. Thank you very much.

Guide : My pleasure.

Key Phrase

· backpack : 배낭(= knapsack, rucksack)
· I didn' t realize that : 그것을 알지 못했습니다.
· (That' s) My pleasure : (도와드리게 되어) 오히려 제가 기쁩니다 .

SCENE 4

Elizabeth : Oh, no, this is not my bag! It looks just like mine, but it isn' t!

Guide : You must have taken the wrong bag off the carousel.

Elizabeth : Yes, and I guess someone else has taken mine. What should do?

Guide : Well, just as soon as we get to the hotel, we' ll call the airport and tell them what' s happened.

Elizabeth : That' s a good idea, thank you.

Key Phrase

· look like mine : 내 것처럼 보이다.
· wrong bag : 잘못된 가방
· must have p.p. ~ : ~했음에 틀림없다.
· I guess ~ : ~라고 생각합니다(= I think).
· as soon as ~ : ~하자마자

[Situation] A tour guide is speaking to Elizabeth who has just discovered that she has lost a document case, containing all her important documents and money.

Elizabeth : I can' t find my travel wallet... I' ve looked everywhere, but it' s missing.

Guide : When did you notice it was missing?

Elizabeth : Well, just now, when I was looking for my room keys.

Guide : What' s in it?

Elizabeth : Well, um. my credit cards – Visa and Amex – my passport and plane ticket. This is terrible!

Guide : Yes, I' ll do what I can to help. The first thing you' ll have to do is to contact the police. They' ll have to make a report.

Elizabeth : What about the credit cards?

Guide : You' ll need to notify your bank at home. You can use the telephone at the hotel to call them. some credit card companies will arrange emergency cash for you.

Elizabeth : Oh, all right. What about the passport? I... I guess I' ll have to call the consulate?

Guide : Yes, their number is in the phone book. I' ll help you find it.

Elizabeth : What about my plane ticket?

Guide : You' ll need to call the airline and explain what' s happened. I' m sure they' ll be able to issue another ticket.

Key Phrase

· document case : 서류가방
· containing ~ : ~을 담고있는
· it' s missing : 분실했습니다.
· (This is) terrible! : 어떻게 해요!
· The first thing you' ll have to do is ~ : 당신이 먼저 해야하는 것은 ~
· arrange : 마련하다, 배열하다.
· emergency cash : 긴급 현금
· consulate : 영사관
· issue : 발행하다.

II

항공기내에서

II

PRACTICAL TRAVEL & AVIATION ENGLISH

Part II

on board

승무원

승무원은 각 항공사를 대표하는 최고의 전문 서비스인이다. 건강한 체력과 세련된 국제 매너, 직업에 대한 프로 의식을 기본으로 갖추고 민간 외교관의 역할을 하는 서비스 산업의 대표자이다.

Smile	서비스의 시작은 미소입니다. 미소는 승객을 편안하게 모시는 마음입니다.
Technique	전문적으로 숙련된 기술이 필요합니다. 기술은 오랜 기간 교육과 자신의 노력으로 갖출 수 있습니다.
Emotion	승객을 감동의 세계로 안내해야 합니다. 승무원은 감동을 만드는 창조의 사람들입니다.
Wisdom	지혜는 삶의 위기에서 구해주는 요술 방망이입니다. 요술 방망이는 승무원의 필수 휴대품입니다.
Attraction	자신만의 개성 있는 매력을 갖추어야 합니다. 승무원은 나라의 얼굴이며 우리들의 기쁨입니다.
Rapidity	승객의 다양한 요구에 신속한 응대가 필요합니다. 기내서비스는 적시의 타이밍이 가장 중요합니다.
Delicacy	섬세하게 서비스하는 자세가 중요합니다. 승무원의 손으로 만드는 서비스가 서비스의 질을 좌우합니다.
Elegance	우아함은 여성의 아름다움입니다. 우아함의 자태를 지닌 사람들의 서비스는 아름답습니다.
Smartness	기내 서비스는 늘 예측 안되는 상황들이 많습니다. 영리함은 여러 가지 상황의 판단 능력을 키워줍니다.
Sincerity	고객은 처음부터 마지막까지 성실함으로 접대해야 합니다. 언제나 처음과 같은 성실함은 서비스만족의 기초입니다.

1. 환영

Good morning, ladies and gentlemen!
On behalf of captain Thomas and the entire crew, welcome aboard Korean Air, a member of Skyteam, flight 901 bound for Toronto via Vancouver. Today, we are delayed due to bad weather. Our flight time to Vancouver will be 11 hours and 30 minutes after take-off. Please refrain from smoking at any time in the cabin or in the lavatories. Also, the use of portable electronic devices is not allowed during take-off and landing. On this flight, we have a Tokyo-based cabin crew on board. If there is anything we can do to make your flight more comfortable, our cabin crew are happy to serve you. Please enjoy the flight. Thank you.

Word Study

· allow : 허락하다.
· On behalf of ~ : ~대신하여
· delay : 지연시키다.
· due to ~ : ~로 인하여
· lavatory : 화장실
· comfortable : 편안한
· portable: 휴대용의
· electronic : 전자의
· device : 장치
· take-off : 이륙
· landing : 착륙
· Tokyo-based : 도쿄를 근거지로 근무하는
· we have someone on board : (누가) 탑승하고 있다.
· refrain from ~ : ~을 삼가다.
· be happy to do ~ : 즐겁게 ~하다.
· make ~ + 형용사 : ~을 (어떠한 상대로) 만들다.
· make ~ more comfortable : ~을 더 편하게 하다.
· cabin crew : 승무원

2. 환영

Good morning, ladies and gentlemen.
On behalf of captain James and the entire crew, it is our pleasure to welcome you aboard Korean Air flight 707, bound for Hongkong. This is a joint service operated by Korean Air and Japanese Airline. It is a pleasure to have you with us. We are sorry for the delay. Our flight time to Hongkong will be 3 hours and 30 minutes after take-off. Please fasten your seat belt and refrain from smoking during the entire flight.
(R/S JOINING): On this flight, we have a Tokyo-based cabin attendant on board. Our cabin attendants are happy to assist you.
Please enjoy the flight. Thank you.

Word Study

- On befalf of ~ : ~을 대신하여
- flight time to ~ : ~까지의 비행시간
- refrain from smoking : 끽연을 삼가다(금연하다).
- during the entire fight : 전비행에 걸쳐
- joint service : 합동 서비스
- operated by ~ : ~에 의해 운영되는
- we are sorry for the delay : 지연되어 죄송합니다.
- take-off : 이륙
- assist : 도와주다.

3. 환영

Good morning(afternoon), ladies and gentlemen.
On behalf of Korean Air, captain Jackson and your crew, welcome aboard. It is a pleasure to have you with us. Today, we are delayed due to heavy rain. Our flight time to Los Angeles will be 12 hours and 30 minutes after take-off. At this time, please fasten your seat belts. We remind you that smoking and taking pictures are not allowed during the entire flight. Our cabin attendants are happy to assist you. Please enjoy the flight. Thank you.

Word Study

· on behalf of ~ : ~ 대신하여
· Welcome aboard : 탑승을 환영합니다. .
· pleasure : 즐거움
· assist : 도움을 주다.
· be happy to ~ : ~해서 즐겁다(기쁘다).
· remind : 상기시키다, 생각나게 하다.
  cf) remind A of B : A에게 B를 생각나게 하다.
· delay : 지연시키다.
· due to ~ : ~ 로 인하여
· during the entire flight : 전비행에 걸쳐
· are not allowed ~ : ~은 허용되지 않습니다.

4. 항공관제(ATC)

(1) 이륙대기

방송 시점 : 항공관제탑(Air Traffic Control Tower)으로부터 이륙허가 혹은 착륙허가를 기다리고 있을 때 방송한다.

Ladies and gentlemen!
We are waiting for take off clearance from the control tower. We are number 9 in line waiting to take off, and expect to depart in a few minutes. Thank you.

(2) 착륙대기

May I have your attention, please.
We are number 9 in line waiting to land,
A. and expect to land in a few minutes.
B. and will be landing as soon as clearance is given from the control tower.
Thank you.

Word Study

take-off : 이륙
clearance : (항공기의 이착륙) 허가, 재고정리
control tower : 관제탑
air control tower : 항공관제탑
be number 9 in line waiting : 기다리는 줄에서 아홉 번째이다.
May I have your attention, please : 주목해 주십시오.

5. 난기류

Ladies and gentlemen,
We will be passing through turbulence. Please return to your seat and fasten your seat belt. Also, we will be suspending the beverage service. The service will be continued as soon as conditions improve. Thank you.

Word Study

· pass through : 어디를 통과하다.
· turbulence : 기체의 유동, 난기류
· return + 물건 : ~를 되돌려주다.
· return to + 장소 : ~로 돌아가다.
· suspend : (일시적으로) 정지하다, 중지시키다.
· We will be suspending the beverage service.
  → 음료수 서비스를 잠시 중단할 것이다.
· beverage service : 음료수 서비스
· as soon as conditions improve : 상태가 호전되자마자

6. 공항접근

Ladies and gentlemen,
We are approaching Inchon International Airport. We will be preparing for the landing. Your cooperation will be appreciated.
Thank you.

Word Study

· approach : 다가가다.
· prepare for : 대비하다, 준비하다.
· cooperation : 협조
· appreciate : 감사하다.

7. 착륙

Ladies and gentlemen!

We will be landing shortly. Please fasten your seat belt and return your seat back, foot rest, and tray table to the upright position.

Also, please secure your carry-on baggage under the seat in front of you or in the overhead bins. All portable electronic devices must be turned off until the aircraft is parked at the gate.

Thank you for your cooperation.

Word Study

· shortly : 곧, 바로
· upright position : 곧은 자세
· secure : 안전하게 하다.
· carry-on baggage : 휴대물품
· secure your carry-on baggage : 휴대물품을 안전하게 고정시키다.
· portable : 휴대용의
· electronic devices : 전자 장비
· park : 정거하다.
· cooperation : 협조
· seatback : 등받침
· overhead bins : 머리 위 선반

8. 수화물관리

(1) 승객 30~40% 탑승시점

Good morning, ladies and gentlemen, welcome aboard.
Thank you for choosing Korean Air. For your comfort and safety, please use the space under the seat in front of you for your briefcase and heavy articles and place lighter items in the overhead bins. If you need help, just ask us. We are happy to assist you. Thank you.

Word Study

· for your comfort and safety : 편안과 안전을 위하여
· briefcase : 손가방
· comfort : 편안함
· choose : 선택하다.
· safety : 안전
· heavy article : 무거운 물건
· lighter item : 가벼운 물건
· overhead bin : 머리 위 선반
· place something + in(at) ~ : 무엇을 ~에 두다.
· if you need help : 도움이 필요하면
· assist : 도와주다 .

9. 수화물관리

(2) 승객 80~90% 탑승시점

Ladies and gentlemen,
This is Korean Air flight 707 bound for Australia. For your comfort and safety, please use the space under the seat in front of you for your briefcase and heavy articles and place lighter items in the overhead bins. If you need help, just ask us. We are happy to assist you. Thank you.

Word Study

· bound for : (배, 비행기 등이) 행의, 향하여 가는
  cf) outbound : 국외로 나가는
      inbound : 국내로 들어오는
· space : 공간
· in front of ~ : ~ 앞에
· place : (물건을 어디에) 두다.
· We are happy to ~ : ~해서 기쁩니다.

10. 출입문 닫기

Ladies and gentlemen,
This is Korean Air flight 707 bound for Sidney. To all ground staff on board, please deplane now. Thank you.

Word Study

· 비행 : flight
· 지상직원 : ground staff
· 기내의 지상직원에게 알립니다 : To all ground staff on board
· 탑승하여 : on board
· 하기하다 : deplane
· (어디) 행의 : bound for

11. 안전수칙시범

Ladies and gentlemen,
We would like to inform you about the safety features of this aircraft. Your life vest is located under your seat. To put the vest on, slip it over your head, then pull the straps tight around your waist. Just before leaving the aircraft, inflate your life vest by pulling the yellow tabs down. You can also inflate it by blowing into the tubes. Your oxygen mask is in the overhead compartment. [Your oxygen mask is in the seat back in front of you. (DC-10 type)]

When the mask appears, put out your cigarettes, pull the mask toward you and cover your nose and mouth. There are emergency exits on both sides of the aircraft, and all exits are clearly marked. Now, please make sure that your seat belt is securely fastened. To fasten the seat belt, insert the link into the main buckle. To unfasten the seat belt, raise the flap and pull on the link. For further information, please refer to the safety instruction card in your seat pocket. Thank you.

Word Study

· inform : 통지하다, 알려주다. · life vest : 구명조끼
· put on : 입다. · flap : 좌석벨트의 버클의 뚜껑
· slip : (머리위로) 뒤집어쓰다. · tab :고리
· overhead compartment : 머리 위 선반
· inflate : 팽창시키다. · oxygen : 산소
· make sure : 확실하게 하다. · securely fastened : 단단하게 매다.
· be clearly marked : 분명하게 표시되어 있다.
· appear : 나타나다. · put out : 끄다.
· insert : 끼우다, 삽입하다. · emergency exit : 비상구
cf) pull on the link : 연결고리를 잡아당기다.
· safety instruction card : 안전 안내 카드
· for further information : 보다 자세한 정보를 원하면
· refer to ~ : ~을 참조하다.

12. 전자장비

Ladies and gentlemen.
To prepare for take-off, all portable electronic devices such as calculators and laptop computers must be turned off until the seat belt sign goes off.

Word Study

· prepare for : 대비하다
· portable : 휴대용의
· electronic device : 전자장비
· calculator : 계산기
· laptop computer : 노트북 컴퓨터
  cf) desktop computer : 책상용 컴퓨터
· such as(like) ~ : (예를 들어 말할 때 사용) ~와 같은

13. 이륙

Thank you for waiting, ladies and gentlemen.
As we are cleared for take-off, please make sure that your seat belt is securely fastened. Thank you.

Word Study

· thank you for + ~ing : ~에 대하여 감사드립니다.
· take-off : 이륙
· securely : 확실하게, 단단하게
· make sure that ~ : ~를 확실하게 하다.
· clear : 치우다, 암호를 해독하다, 허가하다, 통관절차를 밟다.
· be cleared : 허가되다.

14. 안전벨트

Ladies and gentlemen.
The seat belt sign is now off. For your safety, please keep your seat belt fastened when seated. This is a no-smoking flight. Smoking is not allowed at any time in the cabin or in the lavatories. Your cooperation is appreciated.

Word Study

· seat belt sign : 좌석벨트표시등
· be off : 꺼지다.
· For your safety : 안전을 위해
· keep your seat belt fastened : 좌석벨트를 매십시오.

Ladies and gentlemen.
The seat belt sign is now off. For your safety, please keep your seat belt fastened when seated. This is a no-smoking flight. Smoking is permitted only for those passengers seated in the smoking section when the no-smoking sign is off. Smoking in other sections, aisles and lavatories is not permitted at any time.
Your cooperation is appreciated.

Word Study

· no smoking sign : 금연 표시
· section : 구역
· aisle : 통로
· seated in the smoking section : 금연구역에 앉아있는
· lavatory : 세면장
· be permitted : 허가되다.
· at any time : 어떤 때든지
· cooperation : 협조
· appreciate : 감사하다, 고맙게 생각하다.

15. 작동불능

Ladies and gentlemen.

Due to some problems with the water system, we are unable to serve water. Soft drinks and juice will be served instead. We are very sorry for this inconvenience. Your kind understanding will be appreciated.

Word Study

- malfunction : 고장
- Due to ~ : ~때문에
- water system : 물 공급 시스템
- be unable to : 을 할 수 없다.
- inconvenience : 불편
- appreciate : 고맙게 생각하다, 감상 (음미)하다.
- Your kind understanding will be appreciated.
  → 여러분의 친절한 이해에 감사드립니다.(널리 이해해 주십시오)

16. 비행안내

Ladies and gentlemen.
From the left side of the aircraft, you will see Mt. Halla. We are now flying over Jeju.
Thank you.

Word Study

· pass over : 위를 통과하다.
· from the left(right) side of : 의 왼쪽(오른쪽)에서
· aircraft : 항공기 (비행기, 비행선 기구, 헬리콥터 등의 총칭)
· fly over : 위를 날아가다.

17. 물품 부족

(1) 입국서류(Entry forms)

Ladies and gentlemen!
We find we do not have enough entry forms for passengers entering Beijing. Our ground staff will distribute the forms after arrival. We are sorry for this inconvenience, and your kind understanding will be appreciated.

Word Study

· entry form : 입국서류
· after arrival : 도착 후
· understanding : 이해
· distribute : 분배하다. 나누어주다.
· inconvenience : 불편
· appreciate : 감사하다.
· your understanding will be appreciated : 이해하여 주시면 고맙겠습니다.

(2) 쇼핑백 부족(Shopping bags)

Ladies and gentlemen.
We find we do not have enough shopping bags for passengers having purchased duty-free items on board. They will be distributed after arrival at Inchon International Airport. We are sorry for this inconvenience, and your kind understanding will be appreciated.

Word Study

· purchase : 구입하다.
· duty-free items : 면세품
· on board : 기내에서
· international airport : 국제공항
· for passengers having purchased ~ : ~을 구입하신 승객을 위해

18. 스카이패스 안내

Ladies and gentlemen.
We would like to extend a special welcome to our Sky Pass members. Sky Pass is Korean Air' s frequent flyer program, offering many benefits including free flights and upgrades. The mileage of this flight from Incheon to New York is 800,000 miles. If you wish to join, please ask our cabin attendants. Thank you.

Word Study

· Sky Pass : 대한항공이용 단골고객 회원
  cf) Asiana Bonus Club
· would like to : 무엇하기를 원하다.
· extend a special welcome to : 특별히 환영한다.
· frequent : 빈번한
· frequent flyer cf) frequent customer : 단골 고객
· offer : 제공하다
· benefit : 혜택
· include : 포함하다.
· free flight : 무임 비행
· upgrade : 등급 상향
· mileage : 총마일 수, 주행거리
· join : 참가하다, 합류하다.
· if you wish to join : 가입을 원하시면

19. 기내판매

Ladies and gentlemen.
We will be commencing our sky shopping service. Fine selections of world-famous items such as liquor, cigarettes, perfumes and cosmetics are offered at duty-free prices. For further information, please refer to the shopping guide in your seat pocket. According to the customs regulations of the USA, duty free sales will not be available on the next portion between USA and Canada.
Thank you.

Word Study

· commence : 언급하다.
· selection : 선택
· world-famous : 세계적으로 유명한
· such as : 예컨대
· liquor : 술
· perfumes : 향수
· cosmetics : 화장품
· at duty-free prices : 면세가격으로
· for further information : 보다 자세한 내용은
· refer to : 을 참고하다
· shopping guide : 쇼핑 안내서
· according to ~ : ~에 의하면
· customs regulations : 세관규정
· available : 사용할 수 있는
· sales : 판매량(구매)
· portion : 구간

20. 영화상영

Ladies and gentlemen.
Our feature film today is Die Hard 2, starring Bruce Willis.
The English soundtrack is on channel 2. For better viewing, please lower your window blind. Thank you.

Word Study

· feature film : 주된 영화(장편 영화)
· starring : 주연하는(주인공인)
· soundtrack : 소리부분
· be on channel 2 : 채널2에 있다
· for better viewing : 보다 선명하게 보려면
· lower : 내리다
· lower : (참고) 얼굴을 찡그리다, 날씨가 험악해지다.
· window blind (=window shade) : 창 가리개

21. 발표수정

Ladies and gentlemen.
There is a correction to the previous announcement. The local time in Bangkok is 7:30 A.M., not 7:20 A.M. The weather in Bangkok is misty. Thank you.

Word Study

· correction : 정정, 교정 (동사) correct
· correction to ~ : ~에 대한 정정
· previous : 이전의, 앞의
· local time : 현지시간
· misty : 안개 낀

22. 번개

Ladies and gentlemen.
The captain has informed us that the aircraft has been struck by lightening. However, there has been no damage to the aircraft and we will continue our flight as scheduled. Thank you.

Word Study

· inform someone ~ : ~를 누구에게 알려주다.
  cf) inform ~ of + 구
    inform ~ that + 절
· strike : 치다
  cf) strike – struck – struck
· lightening : 번개
  cf) thunder : 천둥
· be struck by lightening : 번개에 맞다.
· damage : 피해
· continue : 계속하다.
· as it was scheduled : 예정된 대로

23. 헤드폰 수거

Ladies and gentlemen.

We hope you have enjoyed our in-flight entertainment. Our cabin attendants will be collecting headphones from passengers who are leaving this aircraft.

Thank you.

Word Study

· entertainment : 오락
· in-flight : 비행중의
· cabin attendants : 승무원
· collect : 수거하다.
· leave + 장소 : ~를 떠나다.
· leave + 물건 : ~를 남기다.

24. 선회

Ladies and gentlemen.

We are circling over Dallas airport.

A. due to air traffic congestion at this airport.

B. due to dense fog (strong winds, heavy snow).

C. due to a runway closing (fire).

We expect to land in a few minutes. Thank you.

Word Study

· circle : 선회(旋回)하다.
· due to ~ : ~로 인하여
· air traffic : 항공교통
· congestion : 혼잡, 복잡
  cf) mental congestion : 정신적 과로
· dense : 짙은, 밀도가 높은
· dense fog : 짙은 안개
· heavy snow, snow storm : 폭설
· runway closing : 활주로 폐쇄
· expect to ~ : ~할 예정이다.

태풍의 종류

① Typhoon : 태평양 서부에서 발생하는 것
   ex) A typhoon is approaching Chejudo. 태풍이 제주도에 다가오고 있다.
② Hurricane : 멕시코만에서 발생하는 것
   ex) Mexico was struck by a hurricane. 멕시코가 허리케인의 엄습을 받았다.
③ Cyclone : 인도양 방면에서 발생하는 폭풍
   ex) a tropical cyclone 열대성 저기압
④ Willy Willy : 호주 방면에서 발생하는 강풍

25. 도착 안내

Ladies and gentlemen.
For entering Korea, please have your entry documents ready.
Passengers having more than 5,000 USD, or the equivalent in foreign currency must declare that amount on the customs form.
Those passengers connecting with Korean Air flights, please be sure to take all your personal belongings with you when you deplane. Also, you are kindly requested to have your onward boarding pass ready. Thank you.

Word Study

· entry documents : 입국서류
· have entry documents ready : 입국서류를 준비하다.
· more than 5,000 USD : 5,000 미국달러보다 많은
· equivalent : 동등한 액수, 양
· foreign currency : 외화
· declare : 신고하다
· amount : 금액
· customs form : 세관신고서
· connecting : 연결하는
· passengers connecting with Korean Air flights
→ 대한항공으로 갈아타는 승객
· be sure to ~ : 반드시 ~하다.
· personal belongings : 개인소지품
· deplane : 하기하다.
· request : 요구하다.
· be requested to : 무엇하도록 요청된다.
· onward : 앞으로 나아가는
· boarding pass : 탑승권
· onward boarding pass : 연결편의 탑승권

26. 탑승인원 재확인

Ladies and gentlemen.

As there is a discrepancy in the number of

A. passengers on board

B. flight coupons (boarding pass, embarkation cards).

A. Please remain seated until the check has been completed.

B. Please have your ticket (boarding pass, embarkation card) ready to be re-checked.

Your cooperation will be appreciated.

Word Study

- discrepancy : 불일치, 모순, 차이
- discreet : 신중한, 분별력 있는
  cf) discrete : 분리된
- flight coupon : 항공권에서 뜯어낸 회사보관용 회수권
- embarkation card : 출국신고서
  cf) embarkation : 출국
  disembarkation : 입국
- remain seated : 좌석에 앉아있다.
- complete : 완전히, 완료하다, 끝마치다.
- cooperation : 협조
- recheck : 재점검
- have ~ ready : ~을 준비하다.

27. 설문지 작성요청

Ladies and gentlemen.

We would appreciate your taking a few minutes of your time to complete the questionnaire we will distribute. This will help us provide even better service in the future. Thank you.

Word Study

· appreciate : 감사히 여기다.
· complete : 완성시키다.
· questionnaire : 질문지
· distribute : 분배하다.
· provide : 제공하다.
· in the future : 앞으로

28. 사람 찾기

May I have your attention, please.
We have a passenger who lost a wallet in the lavatories. If there is any one who has found this wallet, please contact one of your cabin attendants. Thank you.

May I have your attention, please.
One of our passengers requires medical assistance.
If there is a doctor or nurse available, please contact one of your cabin attendants immediately. Thank you.

Word Study

· page : 사람을 찾다.
· lose a wallet : 지갑을 잃어버리다.
· lavatory : 세면장
· contact : 연락을 주다.
· require :요구하다.
· medical : 의료의
· assistance : 도움
· contact : 접촉, 연락
· immediately : 즉시

29. 통과절차

Ladies and gentlemen.

Transit passengers are requested to obtain a transit card after deplaning and proceed to the transit area. You may leave your hand baggage on board, but please be sure to take your boarding pass, passport and other valuables with you. We will be here for about 40 minutes. Reboarding will be announced in the transit area. And Korea Air sky shopping service will be available on the next portion of our flight between New York and Washington. You will find a shopping guide in your seat pocket. Thank you.

Word Study

- transit passenger : 통과승객
- obtain : 얻다, 획득하다, 받다.
- leave something on board : 기내에 (무엇을) 남겨두다.
- hand baggage : 손가방 등 들고 다니는 짐
- transit : 통과하다
- transit card : 통과카드
- transit area : 통과여객이 대기하는 장소
- proceed to + 장소 : 어디로 나아가다
- be sure to do something : 반드시 … 하세요.
- boarding pass : 탑승권
- passport : 여권
- valuables : 귀중품
- available : 사용할 수 있는
- next portion : 다음 구간
- reboarding : 재탑승

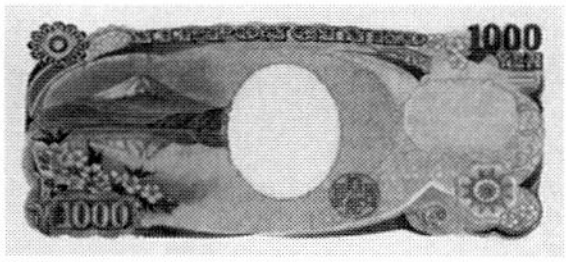

30. 통과절차

Ladies and gentlemen.
Transit Passengers continuing on to Washington are requested to remain on board after arrival. Please refrain from smoking while we are on the ground. We will be here for about 50 minutes. According to customs regulations in New York, all alcoholic beverages and pornographic materials must be collected and secured during our stopover. All items will be returned to you after departure.
Thank you.

Word Study

· transit passenger : 통과승객
· continue on to ~ : ~로 계속하여 여행하는
· remain an board : 내리지 않고
· arrival : 도착
· refrain from smoking : 담배를 삼가다.
· be on the ground : 지상에 있다.
· while ~ : ~하는 동안
· customs regulations : 세관규정
· according to + 명사 : 무엇에 의하면
· alcoholic beverage : 알코올음료
· pornographic material : 음란물
· secure : 안전하게 하다, 고정시키다.
· stopover : 단기체류, 잠깐 들르기
· item : 품목
· return to ~ : ~로 돌아가다.
· departure : 출발

31. 종착역 작별

Ladies and gentlemen.
Welcome to Paris. Today, we are delayed due to heavy snow. The local time is 7:30 in the evening. For your safety, please remain seated until the captain has turned off the seat belt sign. Be careful when opening the overhead bins, and check that you have not left any items behind. We know that you have a choice of airlines and we thank you for choosing Korean Air. It has been our pleasure serving you, and we hope to see you again soon. If you have onward or return bookings with Korean Air, please reconfirm your flight at least 72 hours before your departure. Thank you for flying with us today, and we wish you a pleasant stay here in Paris. Kamsa hamnida.
Thank you.

Word Study

· local time : 현지시간
· for your safety : 귀하의 안전을 위하여
· remain seated : 좌석에 앉은 채로 있다
· turn off : 끄다.
· choice : 선택(cf. choose : 선택하다)
· thank someone for something : 에 대하여 누구에게 감사하다.
· leave items behind : 물품을 뒤에 남겨두고 가다.
· hope to do ~ : ~하기를 희망하다.
· have a choice of ~ : ~의 선택권을 가지고 있다.
· departure : 출발
· booking : 예약(reservation)　　onward booking : 계속편의 예약
· return booking : 돌아가는 편의 예약
· reconfirm : 재확인하다.
· at least : 최소한, 적어도
· thank you for flying Korean Air : 대한항공을 탑승해 주셔서 감사합니다.
· pleasant : 즐거운, 유쾌한

32. 리무진버스 이용

Ladies and gentlemen.
Korean Air offers a limousine bus service every 15 minutes between Incheon Airport and major hotels in downtown Seoul. For more information, please refer to our Morning Calm in-flight magazine, or contact the KAL Limousine service counter at the arrival lounge. Thank you.

Word Study

· offer : 제공하다.
· every 15 minutes : 매 15분마다
· downtown : 도심, 시내
· major : 주요한
· for more information : 보다 자세한 내용은
· magazine : 잡지
· in-flight magazine : 기내잡지
cf) a weekly [monthly] magazine : 주간[월간] 잡지
· refer to ~ : ~을 참고하다.
· Morning Calm : 대한항공 기내잡지 이름
· contact : 연락하다.
· limousine : 전속운전사가 있는 대형고급승용차
· service counter (or desk) : 서비스 안내
· arrival lounge : 도착 여객이 머무는 곳

33. 비행 계획

Ladies and gentlemen.

We would like to inform you of our flight plan today. We will be flying at an altitude of 36,000 feet, with ground speed of 500 miles per hour. Our flight time to Amsterdam will be 15 hours, and we expect to arrive there at 6 A.M., October 10. The time difference between Seoul and Amsterdam is 13 hours. The present time there is 4 p.m., October 9. The weather en route is forecasted to be generally fair. However, we would recommend you to keep your seat belt fastened while seated, as a precaution against turbulence. Thank you.

Word Study

· altitude : (항공기) 고도
  cf) attitude : 태도, 자세
· 36,000 feet : thirty six thousand feet
· ground speed : 대지(對地) 속도
· time difference : 시차
· en route = on the way : 도중에
· forecast : 예보하다, 전조가 되다.
· generally : 일반적으로
· fair : 날씨가 맑은, 공평한
  cf) fare : 운임, 요금
· recommend : 권고하다, 추천하다.
· keep your seat beet fastened : 안전벨트를 착용해 주시기 바랍니다.
· as a precaution against ~ : ~에 대한 대비로서
· turbulence : 기체동요, 난기류

34. 도착 날씨 정보

Ladies and gentlemen.
We will be landing at Incheon Airport in about 10 minutes. The local time is 7 p.m. The weather in Incheon is clear (cloudy, rainy, snowy, fair, hazy) and the temperature is 26 degrees Fahrenheit, 2.2 degrees below Celsius. Thank you.

Word Study

· will be + 진행형 : 곧 무엇할 것이다.
· clear : 맑은
· fair : 쾌청한
· cloudy : 구름 낀
· hazy : 흐린
· temperature : 온도
· Fahrenheit(F) : 화씨의
· Celsius(C) : 섭씨의
· below zero : 영하의
· 20 degrees below : 영하 20도

35. 지상이동

(1) 지상이동 중 회항

Ladies and gentlemen.

We are returning to the parking area,

A. due to technical reasons.

B. because of a sick passenger.

C. at the direction of the control tower.

Further information will be given later.

Your kind understanding will be appreciated.

Word Study

· taxi : 항공기가 지상에서 달리다.
· technical reason : 기술적인 이유
· control tower : 관제탑
· direction : 지시, 방향
· return to ~ : ~로 돌아가다.
· parking area : 주차장, 주기장
· appreciated : 감사하는
· further information : 더 자세한 사항

(2) 지상이동 중 승객 착석 안내

Ladies and gentlemen.

Please remain seated until the plane comes to a complete stop.

Thank you.

Word Study

· remain seated until ~ : ~할 때까지 좌석에서 기다리다.
· come to a complete stop : 완전히 정지하다.
· come to + v ~ : ~한 상태로 되다.

36. 커튼 열고 닫기

May I have your attention, please.
According to the regulations at this airport, all window shades should be closed during take-off, landing and while we are on the ground. Please close your right side window shades now. Your cooperation will be much appreciated.
(AFTER TAKE-OFF)
Thank you for your cooperation, ladies and gentlemen. You may now open the window shades and enjoy your flight. Thank you.

Word Study

· May I have your attention : 알려드리겠습니다.
· according to ~ : ~에 의하면
· regulation : 규칙
· right side : 오른쪽 편
· window shades : 창문 가리개
· be on the ground : 지상에 있다.

37. 도착 후 기내 대기

May I have your attention, please.

The airport authorities have informed us that all passengers are kindly requested to remain on board for about 15 minutes.

A. because of congestion in the immigration / customs area.

B. because of a welcoming / farewell ceremony for honored guests.

Your kind understanding will be appreciated.

(AFTER CLEARANCE)

Thank you for waiting, ladies and gentlemen.

You may now deplane.

Word Study

· authority : 당국(공공기관)
· airport authorities : 공항당국
· request : 요청하다.
· be requested to ~: ~하도록 요청되다.
· congestion : 혼잡, 정체
· immigration : 이민
· customs : 세관
· ceremony : 행사
· honored guest : 귀빈
· clearance : 허가
· deplane : 하기하다. ↔ enplane or emplane

38. 하기지연

Thank you for waiting, ladies and gentlemen.
You may now deplane. Passengers in the back of the cabin, please use the rear door.
Please be careful while deplaning, because it is rainy outside.

Word Study

· rear : 뒤, 후방의 ↔ front
· rear door : 후방에 있는 문
· deplane : 하기하다.
· be careful while deplaning : 하기하는 동안 조심하다.
· snowy/rainy outside : 밖에는 눈이 내리는/ 비가 오고 있는

39. 하기지연

Ladies and gentlemen,

A. We are now waiting for the boarding bridge to be put in position.

B. We are now waiting for the airport shuttle bus.

Please remain seated. Thank you.

Word Study

· be put in position : 완전히 자리를 잡다.
· boarding bridge : 탑승대(항공기와 탑승구를 연결하는 다리)
· shuttle bus : 왕복버스
· remain seated : 자리에 앉아 기다리다.

40. 하기시 후문 이용 안내

May I have your attention, please.
We have some mechanical difficulties in using the front door(trap, bridge). Please deplane through the rear door. Thank you.

Word Study

· rear door : 후문
· mechanical difficulty : 기계적인 문제
· trap : 발판, 사다리
· bridge : 항공기와 탑승구를 연결하는 장치

41. 지연 출발

Ladies and gentlemen.
Due to seasonal tail winds, our flight time to Singapore will be shorter than usual. In order to arrive in Singapore on schedule, we will intentionally delay this flight 1 hour and 20 minutes.

Word Study

· due to ~ : ~로 인하여
· seasonal : 계절적인, 정기적인
· tail wind : 뒤에서 부는 바람
· shorter than usual : 평상시보다 짧은
· In order to ~ : ~하기 위해서
· arrive on schedule : 정시에 도착하다.
· intentionally : 의도적으로

42. 최초 지연

Ladies and gentlemen.

We are waiting for

A. completion of the technical check of this aircraft.

B. completion of baggage loading.

C. departure clearance from immigration authorities.

D. some passengers to board.

E. snow removal from the runway.

F. some connecting passengers to board.

Our departure will be delayed due to

A. unfavorable weather conditions around Incheon Airport.

B. a welcoming / farewell ceremony for honored guests.

(장시간 지연으로 연결편 안내가 필요할 때)

Passengers with inquiries on Korean Air connecting flights after arriving in Incheon, please contact one of your cabin attendants. We expect to depart in about 10 minutes. Your kind understanding will be appreciated.

Word Study

· completion : 완료, 달성 (동사) complete
· technical check : 기술적 점검
· baggage loading : 수하물 적재
· departure clearance : 출발허가
· immigration authority : 출입국 심사국
· snow removal : 제설 (동사) remove
· runaway : 활주로
· unfavorable : 비우호적인, 불리한
· condition : 조건, 상태
· unfavorable weather condition : 불리한 날씨 상태
· honored guest : 귀빈
· ceremony : 의식
· inquiry : 질의
· contact : 연락을 주다.
· depart : 출발하다 (명사) departure

43. 지연: 상태 호전

Ladies and gentlemen.

A. According to the report, the weather conditions around Incheon Airport are now improving.

B. The technical check of this aircraft is almost completed.

Thank you.

Word Study

· according to ~ : ~에 의하면
· improve : 호전되다, 향상시키다.
· aircraft : 항공기(총칭)

44. 지연: 재출발

Thank you for waiting, ladies and gentlemen.

A. As the weather conditions around Frankfrut Am Main Airport have improved,

B. As the technical check of this aircraft has been completed,

we will depart soon. Please recheck your seat belt is fastened.

Thank you.

Word Study

· weather condition : 기상상태
· improve : 향상되다.
· technical check : 기술적 점검
· complete : 완료하다.

45. 지연: 상태 악화

May I have your attention, please.
  A. Our flight will be delayed until tomorrow.
  B. Our flight has been canceled.
    A. because of mechanical failure.
    B. because the weather conditions around Kimhae Airport have become worse.
Beverages (and a snack) will be served shortly.
Passengers are kindly requested to deplane and
  A. wait in the terminal.
  B. follow the guidance of our ground staff.
  C. follow the guidance of our ground staff for further arrangements.
    A. You may leave your baggage on board but please take your passport and other valuables with you.
    B. Please be sure to take all your personal belongings with you.
We are sorry for this inconvenience, and we will keep you informed of further changes.
Your kind understanding will be appreciated.

Word Study

· cancel : 취소하다.
· mechanical failure : 실패, 기계적 고장, 파손
· become worse : 악화되다.
· alcoholic beverage : 알코올성 음료
· terminal : 종착의, 종점, 발착역
· ground staff : 지상직원
· follow : 따르다.
· guidance : 안내
· leave : 남겨두다.
· valuables : 귀중품
· be sure to : 반드시 (무엇) 하다.
· personal belongings : 개인소지품
· keep informed : 알려주다.
· further changes : 앞으로 있을 변화

46. 지연: 탑승 후 재 하기

Ladies and gentlemen.

We are sorry to announce that all passengers are requested to deplane again.

A. because of mechanical failure.

B. because the weather conditions around Cheongju Airport have became worse.

Please wait in the transit area until further information is given.

Thank you.

Word Study

· announce : 알리다.
· be requested to ~ : ~하도록 요청되다.
· weather condition : 기상상태
· transit area : 통과승객이 머무는 장소
· further information : 보다 상세한 내용

47. 음료수 제공

Ladies and gentlemen.

A. We will be serving a snack with soft drinks.

B. Your cabin attendants will guide you to the restaurant.

Thank you.

Word Study

· soft drinks : 가벼운 음료수
· cabin attendant : 승무원
· guide : 안내하다.

48. 착륙후 승객 하기

Ladies and gentlemen.

We have been diverted here in California. The local time is 5 a.m.

(PASSENGER REMAINING ON BOARD)

All passengers are requested to remain on board until further notice. Please refrain from smoking while we are on the ground.

(PASSENGER DEPLANING)

All passengers are requested to deplane and proceed to the waiting lounge and follow the guidance of our ground staff. We are sorry for this inconvenience, and will keep you informed of further changes. Thank you.

Word Study

· diversion : 우회, 회항 (동사) divert
· reroute : 항로를 바꾸다.
· divert : 회항하다, 다른 공항을 향하여가다.
· further notice : 앞으로 있을 안내
· refrain from smoking : 흡연을 삼가다.
· proceed to : 어디를 향하여 나아가다, 진행하다.
· waiting lounge : 대기실
· We are sorry for this inconvenience : 불편을 드려서 죄송합니다.
· will keep you informed of ~ : ~을 알려드리겠습니다.

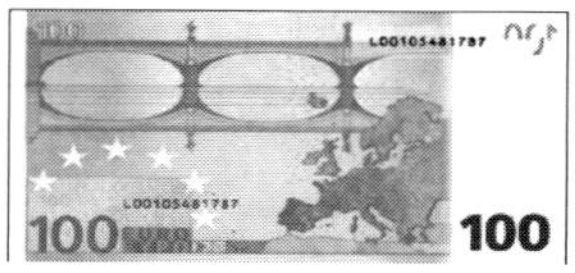

49. 호텔 투숙

May I have your attention, please.

A. Due to a delay in aircraft servicing,

B. Because the weather conditions around San Francisco airport have worsened.

C. Due to heavy fog,

we will be unable to reach San Francisco airport. Therefore we will stay overnight here in L.A.

(CIQ CLEAR)

Please be sure to take all your personal belongings with you and complete customs and immigration clearance here. After clearance, please follow the guidance of our ground staff (cabin attendants). We are sorry for this inconvenience and will keep you informed of further changes. Thank you.

Word Study

· arrival : 도착
· worsen : 악화되다.
· heavy fog : 짙은 안개
· be unable to ~ : ~을 할 수 없다.
· stay overnight : 밤을 새다.
· CIQ CLEAR : 세관, 입국, 검역 허가
  cf) customs, immigration, and quarantine clear
· be sure to ~ : 반드시 ~을 하다.
· personal belongings : 개인 소지품
· after clearance : 통과 후에
· follow guidance : 안내를 따르다.
· inconvenience : 불편
· keep someone informed of ~ : 누구에게 ~을 계속 알려주다.

50. 승객 육로 수송

May I have your attention, please.

A. Due to unfavorable weather conditions around Incheon Airport,

B. Due to a delay in aircraft servicing,

We will be providing ground transportation to your destination.

(CIQ. CLEAR)

Please be sure to take all your personal belongings with you and complete customs and immigration clearance here. Customs inspection for your checked baggage will be done.

(NO CIQ. CLEAR)

Please be sure to take all your personal belongings with you when you deplane. For further information, please ask our ground staff.

Thank you.

Word Study

· aircraft servicing ; 항공기 운행
· unfavorable : 비우호적인
· destination : 목적지
· be sure to ~ : 반드시 ~을 하다.
· weather condition : 기상상태
· ground transportation : 지상교통
· customs inspection : 세관검사
· checked baggage : 검사받은 짐
· immigration clearance : 출입국 허가

51. 비상사태

One minute before landing (or ditching)

One minute before touch down.

Recheck seat belt and adopt the bracing position.

Cradle your head in folded arms, lean on the back of the seat in front of you. Do not relax or unfasten your seat belt until the aircraft has stopped completely.

Word Study

· emergency : 비상
· ditching : 비상착륙
· touch down : 활주로에 항공기의 기어가 닿다, 착지(하다).
· adopt (= assume) : 채택하다, 양자로 삼다.
· assume the emergency landing position
· bracing position : 대비자세를 취하다.
· cradle : 떠받히다, 양손으로 안듯이 들다.
· in folded arm : 팔장을 끼고
· cradle your head in folded arms : 팔을 접어서 머리를 감싸안다.
· lean : 기대다.
· lean on the back of the seat : 좌석의 등에 기대다.
· relax : 늦추다, 힘을 빼다, 긴장을 풀다.
· unfasten : 풀다.

52. 비상사태

(1) 방송할 시간 여유가 있을 때

Attention!
We will have to make an emergency landing in about 10 minutes.
Please remain calm and follow these instructions carefully.
Take out the safety instruction card in your seat pocket.
Put out all cigarettes and fasten your seat belt tight.
Put your personal belongings under your seat.
Remove all sharp objects such as spectacles, dentures, pens and place them in the seat pocket.

(DITCHING)
Take out the life vest located under your seat.
Put on the vest as shown in safety instruction card.
But inflate the vest just before leaving the aircraft.
When the captain orders "Brace for impact", adopt the bracing position shown in the safety instruction card.
Confirm the location of the emergency exit nearest your seat.
There will be more than one impact, so do not relax or unfasten your seat belt until the aircraft has stopped completely.
Follow the directions of the crew who are trained to help you.

(2) 방송할 시간적 여유가 없을 때

Attention!
This is an emergency landing / ditching.
Put out all cigarettes and fasten your seat belt tight!
Cradle your head in folded arms, lean on the back of the seat in front of you.

Word Study

· make an emergency landing : 비상착륙을 시도하다.
· safety instruction card : 안전지시카드
· remain calm : 움직이지 않다.
· instructions : 지시
· personal : 개인의
· belongings : 소지품
· sharp object : 날카로운 물건
· spectacles : 안경
· denture : 의치, 틀니
· inflate : 부풀리다, 팽창시키다 (명사) inflation
· a sense of belonging : 일체감, 소속의식
· brace for the impact : 충격에 대비하다.
· bracing position : 대비자세
· engage in : 종사하다.
· confirm : 확인하다.
· location : 위치
· emergency exit : 비상구
· relax or unfasten : 느슨하게 하거나 풀다.
· direction : 방향, 지시
· crew : 승무원
· be trained to ~ : ~하도록 훈련되어 있다.
· cradle your head in folded arms : 팔을 접어 머리를 감싸다.

53. 작별

Ladies and gentlemen, welcome to Vancouver.

We are sorry for the delay. The local time is 5:55 in the morning. For your safety, please remain seated until the captain has turned off the seat belt sign. When you open the overhead bins, be careful as the contents may fall out. And also please have all your belongings with you when you deplane. Thank you for flying Korean Air, a member of Skyteam, and we wish you a pleasant stay here in Seoul.

Word Study

- local time : 현지시간
- For your safety : 여러분의 안전을 위해
- remain seated : 자리를 떠지 않다.
- turn off : 끄다.
- overhead bins ; 머리위 보관함
- contents : 내용물
- belongings : 소지품

54. 항공사 코드

항공사(약호)	코드	항공사(약호)	코드	항공사(약호)	코드
아메리칸항공(AAL)	AA	에어캐나다(ACA)	AC	에어프랑스(AFR)	AF
안셋호주항공(AAA)	AN	알리탈리아항공(AZA)	AZ	영국항공(BAW)	BA
중국국제항공(CCA)	CA	중국북방항공(CBF)	CJ	캐나다항공(CDN)	CP
캐세이퍼시픽항공(CPA)	CX	중국남방항공(CSN)	CZ	델타항공(DAL)	DL
가루다항공(GIA)	GA	미서부항공(AWE)	HP	고려항공(KOR)	JS
재팬에어시스템(JAS)	JD	일본항공(JAL)	JL	대한항공(KAL)	KE
KLM항공(KLM)	KL	루프트한자항공(DLH)	LH	말레이시아항공(MAS)	MH
중국동방항공(CES)	MU	전일본항공(ANA)	NH	노스웨스트항공(NWA)	NW
에어뉴질랜드항공(ANZ)	NZ	싱가폴항공(SIA)	SQ	러시아항공(AFL)	SU
스위스항공(SWR)	SR	타이항공(THA)	TG	유나이티드항공(UAL)	UA
베트남항공(HVN)	VN	VASP브라질항공(VSP)	VP	월드항공(WOA)	WO
에어인도(AIC)	AI	에어인터항공(ITF)	IT	맥시코항공(MXA)	MX
인도항공(IAC)	IC	이집트항공(MSR)	MS	쿠웨이트항공(KAC)	KU
일본화물항공(NCA)	KZ	아시아나항공(AAR)	OZ	JAT항공(JAT)	JU
이란항공(IRA)	IR	중화항공(CAL)	CI	콘티넨탈항공(COA)	CO
이베리아항공(IBE)	IB	페더럴익스프레스(FDX)	FX	이스라엘항공(ELY)	LY
에바항공(EVA)	BR	핀항공(FIN)	AY	걸프항공(GFA)	GF
거스항공(EIN)	EI	알제리항공(DAH)	AH	쿠바항공(CUB)	CU
나이지리아항공(NGA)	WT	방콕항공(BKP)	PG	LOT 폴란드항공(LOT)	LO
올림픽항공(OAL)	OA	파키스탄항공(PIA)	PK	필리핀항공(PAL)	PR
콴타스항공(QFA)	QF	브리테니아항공(BAL)	BY	오스트리아항공(AUA)	OS
스칸디나비아항공(SAS)	SK	사우디항공(SVA)	SV	남아프리카항공(SAA)	SA
알래스카항공(ASA)	AS	에어포르투갈(TAP)	TP	터키항공(THY)	TK
트랜스월드항공(TWA)	TW	US항공(USA)	US	아르헨티나항공(ARG)	AR
닛뽄항공(ANK)	EL	멕시코항공(AMX)	AM	사베나항공(SAB)	SN

55. 도시 코드

도시명	코드	도시명	코드	도시명	코드
동경	NRT	오사카	KIX	나고야	NGO
후쿠오카	FUK	아오모리	AOJ	히로시마	HIJ
마쓰야마	MYJ	니이가타	KIJ	고마쯔	KMQ
오카야마	OKJ	삿포로	SPK	센다이	SDJ
다카마쓰	TAK	도야마	TOY		
북경	BJS	장춘	CGQ	대련	DLC
광쩌우	CAN	하얼빈	HRB	청도	TAO
상해	SHA	상해	SHE	천진	TSN
연대	YNT				
홍콩	HKG	방콕	BKK	싱가폴	SIN
타이페이	TPE	마닐라	MNL	푸켓	HKT
뉴델리	DEL	호치민	SGN	자카르타	CGK
코타키나바루	BKI	쿠알라룸푸르	KUL	뭄바이	BOM
울란바토르	ULN				
알미티	ALA	하바로프스크	KHV	크라스노야르스크	KJA
모스크바	SVO	타쉬켄트	TAS	블라디보스토크	VVO
사할린	UUS				
로스엔젤레스	LAX	뉴욕	JFK	뉴어크	EWR
샌프란시스코	SFO	시카고	ORD	시애틀	SEA
호놀룰루	HNL	엥커리지	ANC	아틀랜타	ATL
보스턴	BOS				
라스베가스	LAS	올랜도	ORL	필라델피아	PHL
워싱턴	IAD	상파울로	GRU	토론토	YYZ
밴쿠버	YVR				
오클랜드	AKL	브리스베인	BNE	크라이스처치	CHC
괌	GUM	사이판	SPN	시드니	SYD
암스텔담	AMS	프랑프푸르트	FRA	런던	LHR
파리	CDG	로마	FCO	쥬리히	ZRH

56. 공항 코드

코드	공항	나라
ABJ	abijian	C te d' lvoire
ABZ	Aberdeen	UK
ACA	Acapulco	Mexico
ACC	Accra	Ghana
ADD	Addis Ababa	Ethiopia
ADL	Adelaide	Australia
AGP	Malaga	Spain
AKL	Auckland	New Zealand
ALC	Alicacte	Spain
ALG	Algiers	Algeria
AMM	Amman	Jordan
AMS	Amsterdan	Netherlands
ANC	Anchorage	USA
ANK	Ankara	Turkey
ANR	Antwerp	Belgium
ANU	Antigua	Antigua
ARN	Stockholm Arlanda	Sweden
ASU	Asuncion	Paraguay
ATH	Athens	Greece
ATL	Atlanta	USA
AUH	Abu Dhabi	UAE
AXA	Anguilla	Anguilla
BAH	Bahrain	Bahrain
BCN	Barcelona	Spain
BDA	Bermuda	Bermuda
BER	Berlin	Germany
BEY	Beirut	Lebanon
BFS	Belfast	UK
BGI	Barbados	Barbados
BBO	Bergen	Norway
BHX	Birmingham	UK
BIO	Bilbao	Spain
BJL	Banjul	Gambia
BJM	Bujumbura	Burundi
BJS	Beijing	China

코드	공항	나라
BKK	Bangkok	Thailand
BLQ	Bologna	Italy
BNE	Brisbane	Australia
BOD	Bordeaux	France
BOG	Bogota	Colombia
BOM	Bombay	India
BOS	Boston	USA
BRE	Bremen	Germany
BRN	Beme	Switzerland
BRS	Bristol	UK
BRU	Brussels	Belgium
BSL	Basle	Switzerland
BTS	Bratislava	Slovakia
BUD	Budapest	Hungary
BUE	Buenos Aires	Argentina
BUH	Bucharest	Romania
BWI	Baltimore	USA
BZV	Brazzaville	Congo
CAI	Cairo	Egypt
CAS	Casablanca	Morocco
CBR	Canberra	Australia
CCS	Caracas	Venezuela
CCU	Calcutta	India
CDG	Charles de Gaulle	France
CGK	Jakarta	Indonesia
CGN	Cologne	Germany
CHC	Christchurch	New Zealand
CHI	Chicago	USA
CLE	Cleveland	USA
CMB	Colombo	Sri Lanka
CMN	Mohamed V	Morocco
CNS	Caims	Australia
COO	Cotonou	Benin
CPH	Copenhagen	Denmark
CPT	Cape Town	South Africa
CUR	Curacao	Neth. Antilles
CVG	Cincinnati	USA
CWL	Cardiff	UK
DAC	Dhaka	Bangladesh

코드	공항	나라
DAM	Damascus	Syria
DBV	Dubrovnik	Croatia
DCA	Washington National	USA
DCF	Dominica	Dominica
DEL	Delhi	India
DEN	Denver	USA
DFW	Fort Worth	USA
DKR	Dakar	Senegal
DRW	Darwin	Australia
DTT	Detoit	USA
DUB	Dublin	Ireland
DUR	Durban	South Africa
DUS	Dusseldorf	Germany
DXB	Dubai	UAE
EBB	Entebbe	Uganda
EDI	Edinburgh	UK
EMA	East Midlands	UK
EWR	Newark	USA
FAO	Faro	Portugal
FCO	Rome Fiumicino	Italy
FIH	Kinshasa	Zaire
FRA	Frankfurt	Germany
FUK	Fukuoka	Japan
GBE	Gabarone	Botswana
GCI	Guemsey	UK
GCM	Grand Cayman	Cayman Islands
GEO	Georgetown	Guyana
GIB	Gibraltar	Gibraltar
GIG	Rio de Janeiro	Brazil
GLA	Glasgow	UK
GND	Grenada	Grenada
GOA	Genoa	Italy
GOT	Gothenburg	Sweden
GRU	Sao Paulo	Brazil
GEZ	Graz	Austria
GUA	Guatemala City	Guatemala
GVA	Genova	Switzerland
HAJ	Hanover	Germany
HAM	Hamburg	Germany

코드	공항	나라
HAV	Havana	Cuba
HEL	Helsinki	Finland
HKG	Hong Kong	Hong Kong
HNL	Honolulu	USA
HOU	Houston	USA
HRE	Harare	Zimbabwe
IAD	Wahington Dullas	USA
IAH	Houston Int'l	USA
INN	Innsbruck	Austria
ISB	Islamabad	Pakistan
IST	Istanbul	Turkey
JED	Jeddah	Saudi Arabia
JER	Jersey	UK
JFK	Kennedy Int'l	USA
JKT	Jakarta	Indonesia
JNB	Johannesvurg	South Africa
KEF	Reykjavik	Iceland
KHI	Karachi	Pakistan
KIN	Kingston	Jamaica
KLU	Klagenfurt	Austria
KOJ	Kagoshima	Japan
KRT	Khartoum	Sudan
KUL	Kuala Lumpur	Malaysia
KWI	Kuwait	Kuwait
LAD	Luanda	Angola
LAS	Las Vegas	USA
LAX	Los Angeles	USA
LBA	Bradford	UK
LCA	Lamaca	Cyprus
LCY	London City	UK
LED	St. Petersburt	Russia
LEJ	Leipzig	Germany
LGA	La Guardia	USA
LGW	London Gatwick	UK
LHR	London Headthrow	UK
LIL	Lille	France
LIM	Lima	Peru
LIN	Milan	Italy
LIS	Lisbon	Portugal

코드	공항	나라
LJU	Ljubljana	Slovenia
LLW	Lilongwe	Malawi
LNZ	Linz	Austria
LOS	Lagos	Nigeria
LPA	Gran Canaria	Spain
LPB	La Paz	Bolivia
LPL	Liverpool	UK
LTN	Luton	UK
LUN	Lusaka	Zambia
LUX	Luxembourg	Luxembourg
LYS	Lyons	France
MAA	Madras	India
MAD	Madrid	Spain
MAN	Manchester	UK
MBA	Mombasa	Kenya
MCI	Kansas City Int' l	USA
MCO	Orlando	USA
MCT	Muscat	Oman
MEL	Melbourne	Australia
MEX	Mexico City	Mexico
MIA	Miami	USA
MIL	Milan	Italy
MKC	Kansas City	USA
MLA	Malta	Malta
MLW	Monrovia	Liberia
MME	Teeside	UK
MNL	Manila	Philippines
MOW	Moscow	Russia
MPM	Maputo	Mozambique
MQS	Mustique	Grenadines
MRS	Marseilles	France
MRU	Mauritius	Mauritius
MSP	St. Paul	USA
MSY	New Orleans	USA
MUC	Munich	Germany
MVD	Montevideo	Uruguay
MXP	Milan	Italy
NAP	Naples	Italy
NAS	Nassuau	Bahamas

코드	공항	나라
NBO	Nairobi	Kenya
NCE	Nice	France
NCL	Newcastle	UK
NGO	Nagoya	Japan
NOU	Noumea	New Caledonia
NRT	Tokyo Narita	Japan
NUE	Nuremburg	Germany
NYC	New York	USA
ORD	Chicago O' Hare	USA
ORK	Cork	Ireland
ORL	Orlando	USA
ORY	Orly	France
OSA	Osaka	Japan
OSL	Oslo	Norway
OTP	Bucharest Otopeni	Romania
PAR	Paris	France
PBM	Paramaribo	Surinam
PDX	Portland	USA
PEK	Beijing	China
PER	Perth	Australia
PHL	Philadelphia	USA
PHX	Pheonix	USA
PIT	Pittsburgh	USA
PLH	Plymouth	UK
PMI	Palma de Mallorca	Spain
POM	Port Moreby	Papua New Guinea
POS	Port of Spain	Trinidad
PPT	Papeete	French Polynesia
PRG	Prague	Czech Republic
PSA	Pisa	Italy
PTY	Panama City	Panama
RAR	Rarotonga	Cook Islands
REK	Reykjavik	Iceland
ROI	Rio de Janeiro	Brazil
RIX	Riga	Latvia
ROM	Rome	Italy
RTM	Rotterdam	Netherlands
RUH	Riyadh	Saudi Arabia
SAH	Sana' a	Yemen

코드	공항	나라
SAN	San Diego	USA
SAO	Sao Paulo	Brazil
SCL	Santiago	Chile
SEA	Seattle	USA
SEL	Seoul	Korea
SFO	San Francisco	USA
SHA	Shanghai	China
SHJ	Sharjah	UAE
SIN	Singapore	Singapore
SKG	Thessaloniki	Greece
SLC	Salt Lake City	USA
SLU	Saint Lucia	Saint Lucia
SNN	Shannon	Ireland
SOF	Sofia	Bulgaria
SOU	Southampton	UK
STL	Saint Louis	USA
STN	London Stansted	UK
STO	Stockholm	Sweden
STR	Stuttgart	Germany
SVG	Stavanger	Norway
SVO	Sheremetevo	Russia
SVQ	Seville	Spain
SXB	Strasbourg	France
SXF	Schonfeld	Geramny
SYD	Sydney	Australia
SZG	Salzburg	Austria
TCI	Tenerife	Spain
TGU	Tegucigalpa	Hondras
THF	Berlin Tempelhof	Germany
THR	Tehran	Iran
TLL	Tallinn	Estonia
TLS	Toulouse	France
TLV	Tel Aviv	Israel
TPA	Tampa	USA
TPE	Taipei	Taiwan
TRN	Turin	Italy
TUN	Tunis	Tunisia
TYO	Tokyo	Japan
UIO	Quito	Ecuador

코드	공항	나라
VCE	Venice	Italy
VIE	Vienna	Austria
VLC	Valencia	Spain
VNO	Vilnius	Lithuania
WAS	Washington DC	USA
WAW	Warsaw	Poland
WDH	Windhoek	Namibia
WLG	Wellington	New Zealand
YEA	Edmonton	Canada
YEG	Edmonton Int'l	Canada
YMQ	Montreal Mirabel	Canada
YOW	Ottawa	Canada
YTO	Toronto	Canada
YUL	Montreal Dorval	Canada
YVR	Vancouver	Canada
YWG	Winnipeg	Canada
YYC	Calgary	Canada
YYZ	Lester Pearson	Canada

III

외국여행지에서

III

PRACTICAL
TRAVEL & AVIATION
ENGLISH

Part III

at a foreign sights

1. 입국심사

Dialogue

Immigration Officer : Good Evening. Where did you come from?

Byeong-Heon : Seoul, Korea.

Immigration Officer : May I see your passport and form I-94, please?

Byeong-Heon : Here you are.

Immigration Officer : What' s the purpose of your visit?

Byeong-Heon : Business.

Immigration Officer : How long are you going to stay in the United States?

Byeong-Heon : 7 days.

Immigration Officer : Do you have a return airplane ticket?

Byeong-Heon : Yes, here it is.

Immigration Officer : Enjoy your trip.

Byeong-Heon : Thanks.

Key Expression

1. Where did you come from? 이라고 하면 상대방의 국적을 묻는 질문으로서 다른 형태로는 What' s your nationality? 또는 Which country are you from? 등이 있다.
2. 입국 신고서는 disembarkation card나 또는 Form I-94 라고 한다.
3. What' s the purpose of your visit? 에 대한 대답으로는
   · I' m here as a tourist. (관광객으로 왔습니다.)
   · For sightseeing. (관광이요.)
   · Visiting relatives. (친척방문이 목적입니다.)
   · Seeing my daughter/son. (딸/아들을 보러 왔습니다) 등이 있다.
4. 만약 이민국 관리가 미국 내 묵을 숙소를 묻는다면 (Where will you be staying in the U. S.?) 다음과 같이 대답할 수 있다.
   · I' ll stay at the Hilton Hotel. (Hilton 호텔에 묵을 겁니다.)

· I' ll stay with a friend in New York. (뉴욕의 친구 집에 묵을 겁니다.)

· I' ll be staying with my sister' s family. (여동생 집에 묵을 겁니다.)

5. 그밖에 가능한 질문으로는

· What' s your final destination? (마지막 목적지가 어디입니까?)

· Is this your first trip to the U. S.? (이번이 첫 번째 미국여행입니까?)

Word Study

· return air-plane ticket 귀국 항공권
· passport 여권
· immigration inspection 입국심사
· immigration officer 이민국 관리
· Birth date (date of birth) : 생년월일
· Family name (last name) : 성(姓)
· First name : 이름
· Home address (present address) : 현주소
· Nationality (country of citizenship) : 국적
· Occupation : 직업
· Employer : 회사명
· Place of birth : 출생지

Exercise 1

When do you start work?
(A) She started late yesterday.
(B) Whenever you' re ready
(C) You have to undergo training.

2. 수화물취급

Dialogue

Schwarzenegger : Excuse me. where is the baggage claim area for KE 081?

Officer : The baggage claim area is down stairs, and it' s number 3.

Schwarzenegger : Can you help me with finding my baggage?

Officer : Sure.

Schwarzenegger : Thank you.

Schwarzenegger : Excuse me. I can' t find my luggage.

Officer : What was your flight number?

Schwarzenegger : Korean Air, KE 081. All the bags came off the baggage claim, but my bag is missing.

Officer : What sort of bag is it?

Schwarzenegger : One large black suitcase.

Officer : Does it have your name and address on it?

Schwarzenegger : Yes, it does.

Officer : I' ll check it out for you. Can you fill out this form? Description of contents, flight number, and the place you' re staying etc.

Schwarzenegger : O.K.

Officer : I' ll contact you as soon as I locate your baggage.

Key Expression

1. 짐을 'baggage' 또는 'luggage' 라고도 한다.
2. 'the baggage(luggage) claim area' 는 수화물 찾는 곳을 말하며 각 각의 컨베이어 위에는 도착한 항공편이 표시되어 있어 탁송된 수화물을 쉽게 찾을 수 있다.
3. "come off"는 '(물건 등이) 나오다' 의 뜻으로 여기에서는 수화물 컨베이어에서 짐이 나오는 것을 말한다.
4. "Cany ou fill out this form"에서 "fill out"은 '(돛 따위를 활짝) 부풀리다', '커지다, 살찌

다' 등의 뜻이 있으며 여기에서는 '(서식, 문서 등의) 빈 곳을 채우다' 의 뜻으로 쓰였다.

5. "I locate your baggage"에서 "locate"는 '~의 위치를 정하다', '~에 있다', '거주하다' 등의 뜻을 가진 동사로서 여기에서는 '찾아내다', '위치를 알아내다' 라는 뜻으로 쓰였다.

6. 제 수화물을 찾을 수 없어요.

   · I can' t find my baggage (luggage).

   · My baggage is missing.

   · My bag hasn' t arrived yet.

7. 어떤 종류(모양)의 수화물입니까?

   [What kind (sort) of baggage (bag) is it?]

   · It' s a red bag. (붉은 색 가방입니다.)

   · It' s a blue suitcase. (푸른색 여행가방입니다.)

   · It' s a large brown one. (큰 갈색 가방입니다.)

Word Study

· baggage claim tag : 수화물 확인증
· conveyor : 운반장치
· suitcase : 여행가방

Exercise 2

When did you receive your promotion?
(A) I was promoted to sales manager.
(B) Just this morning.
(C) At 4 o' clock tomorrow afternoon.

Exercise 3

Who' s giving presentation this afternoon?
(A) Sam has given me a lot of presents.
(B) Sally spoke to me this morning.
(C) I think it' ll be Dave from sales.

3. 세관통과

Dialogue

Customs Officer : Do you have anything to declare?
Sharon Stone : I have nothing to declare.
Customs Officer : Would you please show me your customs declaration form?
Sharon Stone : Yes. here you are
Customs Officer : Would you please put your suitcase on this table?
Sharon Stone : Sure.
Customs Officer : Ma' am, would you open your suitcase?
Sharon Stone : Certainly.
Customs Officer : What' s in this box?
Sharon Stone : It' s a doll, a gift for my nephew.
Customs Officer : What' s in this bottle?
Sharon Stone : It' s powdered red pepper.
Customs Officer : How much money do you have?
Sharon Stone : I have three thousand U.S. dollars and five hundred thousand Korean won.
Customs Officer : Is this all you have?
Sharon Stone : Yes, that' s all I have.
Customs Officer : Thank you for your time. You may go now.

Key Expression

1. "What is this?" (이것은 무엇입니까?)에 대한 대답으로는
   · It' s for my personal use./It' s my personal property.
   (제가 쓰는 개인용품입니다.)
   · This is a souvenir/gift for my friend.
   (목걸이가 하나있는데 친구에게 줄 선물입니다.)

2. 가지고 온 돈에 대한 대답으로는

I have six hundred U.S. dollars in cash and two thousand five hundred dollars in traveler' s check.

(현금 600달러와 여행자 수표 2,500달러가 있습니다.)

3. Do you have anything to declare? (신고할 사항이 있습니까?)에 대한 대답으로는

· No, I have nothing to declare.

(아니오, 아무 것도 없습니다.)

· Yes, I have something to declare.

(예, 신고 할 사항이 있습니다.)

· Yes, I have two bottles of whisky/wine.

(위스키/포도주 두 병이 있습니다.)

4. 그 물건의 가격은 얼마인가요? (What' s the value of it?)

이 물건은 세금을 내셔야 합니다. (You have to pay duty on this.)

술이나 담배가 있습니까? (Do you have any liquor or cigarettes?)

· I have just one carton of cigarettes but no liquor.

(담배 1상자(10갑)만 있고 술은 없습니다.)

· Just one bottle of cognac.

(코냑 한 병만 있습니다)

5. 과일이나 야채가 있나요? (Are you carrying any fruits or vegetables?)

과일반입은 금지되어 있습니다. (You' re not allowed to bring fruits.)

Word Study

· Anchovy : 젓갈류(멸치)

· Dried Seafood : 어포류

· Seaweeds : 김

· Pottery Ceramics : 도자기류

· Beanpaste mixed with red pepper : 고추장

· duty-free articles : 면세품

· prohibited articles : 반입금지품

· customs duty : 관세법

· quarantine : 검역

· vaccination certificate : 예방접종증명

· customs inspection : 세관검사

4. 환전

Dialogue

Bank Teller : May I help you, sir?

Dicaprio : I' d like to cash this traveler' s check.

Bank Teller : Certainly. May I see your passport?

Dicaprio : All right. Here you are.

Bank Teller : Please fill out this form and please sign at the bottom of the check.

Dicaprio : Sure.

Bank Teller : How much money would you like to exchange?

Dicaprio : I' d like to change four hundred dollars.

Bank Teller : How would you like it?

Dicaprio : 2 hundred-dollar bills, 8 twenty-dollar bills, 3 ten-dollar bills and 2 five-dollar bills, please.

Bank Teller : Now, here' s your money.

Key Expression

1. '~을 ~으로 교환하다' 라는 표현은 'exchange ~ for' 외에 'change ~ into/for' 로 쓸 수 있다.
2. 환전할 때 'How would you like it?' 란 것은 '어떤 종류의 지폐로 드릴까요?' 라는 뜻이다.
3. '얼마짜리 몇 장' 이라는 표현은 '2 hundred-dollar bills' (100달러짜리 2장) 외에 '2 hundreds' (100달러짜리 2장) '4 twenties' (20달러짜리 4장) '6 tens' (10달러짜리 6장) 등으로 표현할 수 있다.
4. 호텔 정보에 관한 또 다른 표현으로는 'Can you recommend a hotel?' 'Will you please give me information of hotels?' 'Could you suggest a hotel, please?' 'May I have a list of hotels?'
5. 지역정보에 관한 표현으로는 'Can you recommend some places of interest around here?' (이 부근의 관광 명소를 소개해 주실 수 있나요?)

· 가까운 은행이 어디인가요?
(Where is the nearest bank?)
· 여기에 사인해 주시겠어요.
(Please sign your name here.)
· 여행자 수표를 보여주시겠습니까?
(May I see your traveler' s check, please?)
· 잔돈으로 바꿔주세요.
(Will you break this into small change?)
· 수수료는 얼마인가요?
(How much commission do you charge?)
· 버스시간표가 있나요?
(Can I have a bus timetable?)
· 약도를 그려 주시겠어요?
(Could you draw me a map?)

Word Study

· currency : 통화
· bill : 지폐
· quarter : 25센트 동전
· nickel : 5센트 동전
· buck : 1달러
· cash : 현금
· exchange rate : 환율
· dime : 10센트 동전
· penny : 1센트 동전

Exercise 4

Why did you leave the light on in the office?
(A) Susan' s still working in there.
(B) I turned them on when I came in.
(C) It' s dark in here in the house.

5. 교통편 이용

Dialogue

Rental staff : What can I do for you?

Michelle : I' d like to rent a car, please.

Rental staff : How many days would you like to use it?

Michelle : About a week.

Rental staff : Which size of car would you like?

Michelle : A medium-sized car, please.

Rental staff : A Mercury Sable is available for now.

Michelle : O.K. How much does it cost for a week?

Rental staff : 240 dollars for a week with unlimited mileage.

Michelle : How about the insurance?

Rental staff : Do you have your own insurance?

Michelle : No.

Rental staff : O.K. If you want full cover insurance, it will be three dollars per day. Is there any additional driver?

Michelle : No.

Rental staff : May I have your driver' s license, please?

Michelle : Is the international driver' s license fine?

Rental staff : Sure.

Key Expression

1. 자동차 사이즈에는 소형(small/compact), 중형(medium/mid-sized), 대형(luxury) 등이 있다.
2. 'unlimited mileage' 는 마일 수 제한이 없는 것을 말하며, 하루에 200mile(320km)이내의 제한을 둔다면 가격이 10달러 정도 저렴하다.
3. 'insurance' 는 자동차 보험을 말하며, 개인이 자동차보험을 가지고 있다면 따로 보험을 사지않고 기존 자신의 보험으로 추가 비용 없이 차를 빌릴 수 있다.

4. ‘additional driver’ 란 본인을 제외한 다른 운전자를 말하며, 만약에 친구와 번갈아 운전할 계획이라면 추가 운전수당 얼마씩 비용을 지불해야 만약 사고가 나더라도 보상을 제대로 받을 수 있다.
5. 외국인은 국제면허증(International driver’ s license)이 있어야만 차를 빌릴 수 있으며 미국에서 운전 경험이 없다면 차를 빌리는 것은 신중히 고려해서 결정하는 게 바람직하다.

· 이 버스가 힐튼호텔에 갑니까?
(Does this bus stop at the Hilton hotel?)
· 버스에 타세요.
(Get on the bus.)
· 여기서 내려주세요.
(Let me off here, please. / I’ m getting off.)
· 언제 내릴지 알려 주시겠습니까?
(Would you please tell me when should I get off?)
· 뉴욕 행 버스는 몇 분마다 운행합니까?
(How often does the bus run for New York?)
· 버스를 잘못 타셨습니다.
(You are on the wrong bus.)
· 택시 승차장은 어디입니까?
(Where can I catch a taxi?)
· 어디로 모실까요?
(Where can I take you?)
· 이 근처에 지하철역이 있나요?
(Is there a subway station around here?)
· 월스트리트에 가려면 어느 노선을 타야 하나요?
(Which line should I take to get to Wall Street?)

Word Study

· bus route map : 버스 노선표 · rental agreement : 대여 계약서

6. 투숙

Dialogue

Receptionist : What can I do for you?
Emmanuel : Do you have a room available for tonight?
Receptionist : What kind of room would you like, a double room or single room?
Emmanuel : A double room, please.
Receptionist : Just one night, sir?
Emmanuel : Yes.
Receptionist : Let me see. I' m sorry, sir. There is no double room available for tonight. Only a twin room is available.
Emmanuel : That' s all right. How much is it?
Receptionist : 50 dollars per night plus tax, including a breakfast.
Emmanuel : When is breakfast time?
Receptionist : Six to nine. How would you pay for it, cash or charge?
Emmanuel : Do you take traveler' s checks?
Receptionist : Of course, we do. Would you fill out this form, please?
Emmanuel : Sure.
Receptionist : This is the key for room 707 and your check-out time is twelve noon.
Emmanuel : Thanks.

Key Expression

1. 방을 구한다는 또 다른 표현은 "Can I have a room, please?" 또는 "May I have a room please?" 또는 "Is there a room available tonight?" 등이 있다.
2. 'double room' 이란 2인용 객실로 넓은 더블 베드가 1개 있는 것을 말하며, 'twin room' 은 역시 2인용 객실이지만 싱글 베드가 2개가 있는 것을 말한다. 참고로 'single room' 은 침대가 하나있는 1인용 객실을 말하며, 'triple room' 은 싱글 베드가 3개인 3인용 객실을 말한다. 'suite room' 은 응접실과 침실이 함께 있는 특실을 말한다.

3. 오늘 밤 방을 하나 예약할 수 있을까요? (Can I make a reservation for tonight?)

· 5일간 묵고 싶습니다.
(I'd like to stay for five days.)
· 하루에 얼마입니까?
(What's the rate for a room per night?)
· 요금에 아침식사가 포함됩니까?
(Does the price include breakfast?)
· 좀 더 싼 방이 있나요?
(Are there any cheaper rooms?)
· 싸고 깨끗한 방이 있나요?
(Is there a cheap and clean room?)

Word Study

· reservation : 예약
· concierge : 호텔안내인
· manager : 지배인
· registration card : 숙박 카드
· maid : 여자청소부
· bill : 계산서

Exercise 5

Can I get a quote on the new model?
(A) Check their bank receipts.
(B) Refer to the price list.
(C) Use their computer program.

Exercise 6

Will you have time to fix my printer today?
(A) I don't think so; I'm pretty busy.
(B) If you can't finish it, let me know.
(C) I never said anything like that to him.

7. 룸서비스 이용

Dialogue 1. 아침식사 주문

Bellman : Good morning, How can I help you?

Sandra : I' d like to order a breakfast.

Bellman : O.K. What would you like to order?

Sandra : I' d like two scrambled eggs with two sausages, coffee and orange juice, please.

Bellman : All right. What' s your room number?

Sandra : 505

Bellman : Thank you. Is there anything else you need?

Sandra : Would you also bring me some ice and water, please?

Bellman : Sure. We' ll bring them up right away.

Dialogue 2. 비즈니스 서비스

Steven : Excuse me. I' d like to make some photo copies.

Concierge : Sure. How many copies would you like to have?

Steven : Just two copies of this document.

Concierge : O.K.

Steven : And, is there a business room in the hotel? Actually, I' d like to send some e-mails.

Concierge : Of course. On the second floor there is a business room and you can send your e-mails there.

Steven : Thanks a lot.

Key Expression

1. 계란의 요리 방법에는 boiled egg(삶은 계란), scrambled egg(계란을 풀어서 익힌 것), fried egg(프라이팬에 익힌 것)가 있는데, fried egg에는 easy over(계란 양쪽을 익힌 것)와 sunny-

side up(한쪽만 익힌 것)이 있다.

2. 복사를 부탁한다는 말의 다른 표현들에는 'Can I make some photo copies?' 또는 'Can you take a copy of this document?' 또는 'Can I have copy services?' 등이 있다.
3. 호텔에는 비즈니스 룸이나 회의실(conference room)등이 갖추어져 있어 각종 복사기나 팩스, 컴퓨터 등을 이용할 수 있고 각종 회의도 열 수 있다.

· I need some soap / shampoo / bath towels.
(비누 / 샴푸 / 목욕수건이 필요합니다.)
· Do you have laundry services?
(세탁 서비스를 받을 수 있나요?)
· I want to get my suit cleaned by tomorrow.
(내일까지 양복을 크리닝 해주세요.)
· Would you keep these valuables for me?
(이 귀중품들을 맡아 주실 수 있나요?)
· Is there a fitness center?
(헬스클럽이 있나요?)
· What time does the restaurant open?
(식당은 언제 문을 엽니까?)
· I lost room key.
(방 열쇠를 잃어버렸습니다.)

Word Study

· laundry : 세탁물
· trousers : 바지
· toilet paper : 휴지
· suit : 양복
· xerox : 복사기
· soap : 비누

Exercise 7

Where did you get these statistics from?
(A) I don' t know how to calculate that.
(B) They interviewed several witnesses.
(C) Bush calculated them for us.

8. 시간 약속

Dialogue 1. 약속장소 도착

David : Excuse me.

Susan : Yes?

David : Hello, my name is David Brown. I have an appointment with Ms. Hannah Johnson.

Susan : Oh! Mr. Brown. How are you? Ms. Johnson is waiting for you. Would you follow me, please?

David : Thanks.

Hannah : Mr. Brown. How are you?

David : Good. How are you today?

Hannah : All right. So, how was your flight? Wasn' t it terrible? I hate flying.

David : Well. not too bad. Actually, it was a short trip indeed.

Hannah : O.K. Let' s talk about the business.

Dialogue 2. 전화로 시간 약속

Phil : Hello, This is Dr. Barry' s office.

John : Hi. My name is John, and would it be possible to make an appointment with Dr. Barry?

Phil : One moment, please. I' ll check his schedule. Is 4:00 p.m. tomorrow all right?

John : No, I' m sorry. I' m afraid 4:00 p.m. isn' t suitable. What about 2:00 p.m?

Phil : Great. That will be fine.

John : O.K. See you then.

Phil : Bye.

Key Expression

1. 'appointment'는 '임명, 지명'이라는 명사의 뜻이 있으며 여기에서는 '(회합, 방문의) 약속'을 의미한다. '약속을 지키다'를 표현할 때는 'keep one's ~'를 쓰며, '약속을 정하다'는 'make an ~'로 표현한다.
2. '시간 약속을 하고 싶습니다'의 다른 표현에는 'I'd like to make an appointment. / I want to make an appointment. / Can I make an appointment?'가 있다.

· I'd like to confirm my appointment with Mr. Kim.
(김 씨와의 약속을 재확인하고 싶은데요.)
· I'm terribly sorry but I have to cancel my appointment.
(죄송하지만 약속을 취소하고 싶어요.)
· Can I put off my appointment with Ms. Laura?
(로라 양과의 약속을 연기할 수 있나요?)

Word Study

· appointment : 약속
· confirm : 확인하다.
· cancel / break / call off : 취소하다.
· postpone / defer / put off : 연기하다.

Exercise 8

When do you think you will be finished with the computer?
(A) Maybe in an hour or so.
(B) We finished late last night.
(C) We have several computers.

9. 전화 이용

Dialogue

Operator 1 : Operator. May I help you?

Hyo-ri : I' d like to make an international call to Seoul, Korea.

Operator 1 : Just a moment. I' ll put you through to the international operator.

Operator 2 : International operator. Can I help you?

Hyo-ri : I' d like to make a collect call to Seoul, Korea.

Operator 2 : What' s the number you want to call?

Hyo-ri : The area code is 2, and the phone number is 777-7777.

Operator 2 : What' s your name?

Hyo-ri : My name is Hyo-Ri Lee.

Operator 2 : Who would you like to talk to?

Hyo-ri : Anyone.

Operator 2 : O.K. Hold on. Please, go ahead, Ms. Lee. Your party is on the line.

Hyo-ri : Thanks.

Key Expression

1. 'put through' 는 '~을 꿰뚫게 하다' '(법안따위를) 통과시키다' '~을 도와서 (시험에) 합격시키다' '(일을) 성취하다' 등의 뜻이 있으며 여기에서는 '(~의 전화를) 연결시키다' 라는 뜻으로 쓰였다.
2. 'collect call' 이란 수신자가 요금을 부담하는 전화 방법을 말하며 그 외의 전화 걸기 방법 중에는 위에서 말했듯이 'station call' 'personal call' 등이 있다.

· 국제전화는 어떻게 걸 수 있나요?
(How can I make an international call?)
· 장거리 전화를 걸고 싶습니다.
(I' d like to make a long distance call.)

· 전하실 말씀이 있나요?
(Is there any message?)
· 전화했다고 만 전해주세요.
(Just tell him/her that I called.)
· 전화하라고 말씀드릴까요?
(Shall I ask him/her to call you back?)
· 좀더 크게 말씀해 주실래요?
(Would you speak a little louder?)

Word Study

· station call : 번호통화
· personal call : 지명통화
· local call : 시내전화
· collect call : 수신자 부담 전화
· long distance call : 장거리 전화
· operator : 교환원
· country code : 국가번호
· pay phone : 공중전화

Exercise 9

What' s your sister doing these days?
(A) She is doing very well.
(B) She just started a new job.
(C) She' s in the dining room.

Exercise 10

Which leather coat do you want to buy?
(A) The one on the right.
(B) In this weather you need a coat.
(C) This one' s very expensive.

10. 만남

Dialogue

Peter : Hi. Are you enjoying the party?

Joan : Well, so-so. I' m little bit tired today.

Peter : Do you know the people out there?

Joan : No, not really.

Peter : Now I know why you are tired. Anyway, let me introduce myself. My name is Peter Johnson, and you are?

Joan : Joan, Joan Moore.

Peter : It' s nice to meet you finally. Mike talks about you all the time. You are Mike' s neighbor, aren' t you?

Joan : Nice to meet you, too. I hope you' ve heard only the good things about me.

Peter : Have you lived here long?

Joan : Just 2 weeks.

Peter : Do you like the place?

Joan : Yes, the people around me are very friendly.

Peter : Anyway, just call me Peter, and I' ll introduce you to some of my good friends.

Joan : Thanks. That would be interesting.

Key Expression

1. 3자를 통하지 않고 자신이 직접 남에게 소개하는 표현 중 예의를 갖춘 것에는 'It' s a pleasure to make your acquaintance. My name is …' 나 'I' d like to introduce myself.' 등이 있다. 반면에 편한 표현들에는 'Hi, I' m… Nice to meet you.' 또는 'My name is … and who are you?' 등이 있다.
2. 만나서 반갑다는 표현에는 'It' s a pleasure to meet you.' 또는 'Grad/ Nice to meet you.' 또는 'Pleased to meet you.' 등이 있다.

· 나를 그 사람에게 소개해 주겠어요?
(Would you introduce me to him?)
· 스티브씨 이쪽은 저의 상사 Mr. Lee입니다.
(Mr. Steve, this is my boss, Mr. Lee.)
· 만나기를 고대하고 있었습니다.
(I have been looking forward to meeting you.)
· 말씀 많이 들었어요.
(I' ve heard a lot about you.)

Word Study

· introduce : 소개하다.
· pleasure : 기쁨
· acquaintance : 면식, 교분
· chief : 수장, 우두머리

Exercise 11

How much farther is it to his house?
(A) We' re almost there.
(B) He passed it a minute ago.
(C) We' re running out of time.

Exercise 12

Would you mind opening the window a bit?
(A) The window is closed now.
(B) Sure, it is hot in here.
(C) Windows are on sale now.

11. 식당 이용

Dialogue

Waitress : Good evening. Do you have a reservation?

Dong-min : No, I don' t.

Waitress : O.K. How many, sir?

Dong-min : Four.

Waitress : I' m sorry. Our tables are full right now. Would you wait here for a moment?

Dong-min : About how long should we wait?

Waitress : No more than 5 minutes.

Dong-min : All right. We' ll wait.

Waitress : Now we have a table for you. This way please.

Dong-min : Thank you.

Key Expression

1. '자리가 있나요?' 의 표현에는 'Can we have a table?' 또는 'Is there a table for four?' 등이 있다.
2. '얼마나 기다려야 합니까?' 의 또 다른 표현에는 'How long will it be?' 또는 간단히 'How long.' 등이 있다.

· 요금이 대충 얼마입니까?
(About how much is the fare?)
· 앞으로 얼마 정도 더 걸립니까?
(How much longer will it be?)
· 잔돈은 가지세요.
(Keep the change.)
· 주위에 한국식당이 있나요?

(Are there any Korean restaurants around here?)

· 정장을 해야 합니까?

(Should I be formally dressed?)

Word study

· taxi fare : 택시 요금
· extra fare : 할증 요금
· occupation : 직업
· formally : 형식적인, 정장의

Exercise 13

May I have your driver' s license, please?
(A) No, I' m not sick.
(B) Here it is, officer.
(C) It' s a new car.

Exercise 14

Does flight 707 for London leave from this gate?
(A) Yes, but it won' t board for another hour.
(B) It leaves at 10:45.
(C) It should be on time.

12. 음식 주문

Dialogue

Waiter : What kind of food would you like?

Min-u : I' d like a Whopper combo, please?

Waiter : Would you like it with cheese?

Min-u : Yes, please.

Waiter : What kind of drink would you like?

Min-u : Diet Coke, please.

Waiter : Is that all for you?

Min-u : Yes, that' s all I want.

Waiter : O.K. It' ll be $3.27. Here or to go?

Min-u : For here, please.

Key Expression

1. 'Whopper' 는 햄버거 가게 체인점 중에 하나인 'Burger King' 이란 곳의 메뉴중 하나이고, 'combo' 라고 하면 일종의 세트메뉴로 햄버거, 프렌치 프라이 그리고 음료수 등이 함께 나오는 메뉴를 말합다.
2. 'Diet Coke' 이란 'Coca Cola' 회사의 콜라 종류의 하나로 우리 나라에서는 약간 성격이 틀리긴 하지만 비슷한 종류로 'Light Cola' 가 있다.
3. 'for here' 란 식당에서 먹는 것을 말하며, 'to go' 는 음식을 갖고 가는 것을 말한다.

· 오늘의 특별요리는 무엇입니까?
(What' s today' s special?)
· 시원한 물 한잔 주시겠어요?
(Can I have a glass of iced water?)
· 계산서 좀 주세요.
(Can I have a check (or bill), please?)

Word study

1. 요리법

· baked : 구운
· broiled : 불에 구운
· fried : 기름에 튀긴
· boiled : 삶은
· saute : 살짝 튀긴
· grilled : 석쇠에서 구운

2. 생선 종류

· Bass : 농어
· Codfish / Cod : 대구
· Mackerel : 고등어
· Salmon : 연어
· Shrimp : 새우
· Tuna : 참치
· Clam : 조개
· Lobster : 바다가재
· Oyster : 굴
· Scallop : 가리비
· Swordfish : 황새치
· Trout : 송어

Exercise 15

What time are you leaving for the airport?
(A) I have to leave in a few minutes.
(B) That would be nice.
(C) I certainly hope so.

Exercise 16

Can you give me a ride to the train station?
(A) Of course, I' ll be leaving in a minute.
(B) It could be at least five kilometers.
(C) It' s almost six forty-five.

13. 주점 이용

Dialogue

Bartender : Good evening. What would you like to drink?

Yong-man : A double whiskey, please.

Gyeong-gyu : Get me a Scotch on the rocks.

Bartender : Sure…. Here it is. Is there anything else?

Yong-man : No, thanks.

Gyeong-gyu : May I have another one, please?

Bartender : It' s coming right up.

Yong-man : Excuse me. Check, please.

Bartender : O.K. Would you like one check or separate checks?

Yong-man : One check, please.

Bartender : All right.

Key Expression

1. 'a double whiskey' 라고 하면 정량의 두 배를 주문할 때 쓰는 말이며 'a single whiskey' 는 정량을 주문할 때 쓰인다.
2. 'on the rocks' 는 컵 속에 몇 개의 얼음 덩어리를 넣는 것을 말한다. 그밖에 물이나 소다수를 타서 같이 먹는 것을 'with water or with soda water' 등으로 표현한다.
3. 'come up' 이란 (1) (해 따위가) 오르다, (2) 싹을 내다, (3) 두드러지다, (4) 상경하다 등의 뜻을 가진 관용어구인데 여기에서 'coming right up' 이란 '곧 나타난다' 즉 금방 가져다 준다는 뜻으로 쓰였다.
4. 'separate check' 이란 개개인이 별도로 계산하는 것을 말한다.

· 제가 한 잔 살게요.
(I' ll buy you a drink.)
· 안주가 있습니까?

(Do you have any snacks?)

· 딴 데 가서 한 잔 더 할까요?

(How about another drink at some other place?)

· 봉지를 둘로 나누어 넣어 주실 수 있나요?

(Could you put them in two bags?)

· 담배 한 보루 주세요.

(Could I have a carton of cigarets?)

· 재떨이 좀 갖다 주시겠어요?

(Could you get us an ash tray?)

Word Study

· pack : 꾸러미
· carton : 상자, (담배)한 보루
· vending machine : 자동 판매기
· convenience store : 연중 무휴, 24시간 영업하는 작은 가게
(대표적인 예로 '7-Eleven' 이 있다.)

Exercise 17

Where did you go to school?
(A) At Daewon Science College.
(B) In the 1970' s.
(C) I studied economics.

Exercise 18

Where should we meet for dinner?
(A) It' s in my wallet.
(B) I usually go at one o' clock.
(C) Anywhere you like is fine with me.

14. 우편물 발송

Dialogue 1. 등기 우편물

Clinton : I' d like to send this letter to Korea by registered mail.
Post office staff : All right. Please fill out this form.
Clinton : O.K. Here it is.
Post office staff : That' ll be $3.75.
Clinton : There you go.
Post office staff : Here' s your change.

Dialogue 2. 소포

Hilrary : I' d like to send this parcel to Korea by air.
Post office staff : What' s in it?
Hilrary : There are books.
Post office staff : O.K. Would you fill out the customs card?
Hilrary : Sure.
Post office staff : Let me weigh it. It' ll be $27.45 by air parcel.
Hilrary : Here you are.

Key Expression

1. 'registered mail' 이라 하면 보통 우리나라의 '등기우편' 을 말하며, 그밖에 비슷한 종류로 'certified mail' (배달증명 우편물) 그리고 'Insured mail' (보험을 든 우편물)등이 있다.
2. 'parcel' 이란 '꾸러미, 소포' 를 말하며 비슷한 말로 'package' 가 있다.
3. 'the customs card' 는 외국에 소포를 부칠 때 통관에 필요한 사항을 적은 용지를 말하며, 대개 소포의 내용물이나 소포의 가치를 표시한다.

· 이 소포를 한국에 속달로 보내고 싶습니다.
(I' d like to send this parcel to Korea by express mail.)
· 이 편지를 보내는데 가장 빠른 방법은 무엇인가요?
(What is the fastest way to send this mail?)
· 이 소포에 보험을 들고 싶습니다.
(I' d like to put insurance on this parcel.)
· 보상액은 어떻게 됩니까?
(What is the coverage?)

Word Study

· postcard : 엽서
· parcel : 소포
· envelope : 봉투
· express mail : 속달 우편
· zip code : 우편번호
· postage : 우편요금

Exercise 19

Did you meet John at the party the other night?
(A) We' ve changed it to this Saturday.
(B) Fine, What time did you have in mind?
(C) Was he the really tall one with dark hair?

Exercise 20

How many are you expecting for Roger' s party?
(A) Absolutely. I' m really looking forward to it.
(B) We' ll decide after everyone shows up.
(C) Right now I' d say about ten or fifteen.

15. 길 안내

Dialogue

Mu-hyeon : Excuse me. I think I got lost. What street am I on now?

George : You' re on 35th street.

Mu-hyeon : Will you please tell me the way to the Hilton Hotel? By the way, Can I walk there from here?

George : Well, it' s a long way I guess. You' d better go by taxi or bus.

Mu-hyeon : Could you tell me which bus should I take?

George : Sure. Turn to the right at the first corner, and you' ll find it.

Key Expression

1. 'got lost' 는 (1) 분실하다 (2) 길을 잃다 (3) 열중하다 등의 뜻이 있으며 여기에서는 '길을 잃다' 는 뜻으로 쓰였다.
2. 'had better' 는 '~하는 편이 낫다' 라는 표현으로 구어에서는 'had' 를 생략할 수도 있다.

· 저는 지금 이 지도에서 어디에 있습니까?
(Where am I now on this map?)
· 가장 가까운 지하철역이 어디입니까?
(Where is the nearest subway station?)
· 걸어서 얼마나 걸리나요?
(How long will it take on foot?)
· 관광팜플렛을 얻을 수 있을까요?
(Can I have a tour brochure?)
· 어떤 관광이 있나요?
(What kind of sightseeing tours do you have?)
· 관광 일정에 대해 상세히 설명해 주시겠어요?
(Would you tell me about the tour schedule in detail?)

· 몇 시에 관광이 시작됩니까?
(What time does the tour start?)
· 입장료는 얼마인가요?
(How much is the admission fee?)
· 여기서 사진을 찍어도 되나요?
(Can I take a picture here?)
· 사진을 좀 찍어주세요?
(Could you take a picture for me?)

Word Study

· sightseeing : 관광
· brochure : 팜플렛, 안내책자
· square : 광장
· admission fee : 입장료

Exercise 21

When did he get back from vacation?
(A) She has been workings here for three years.
(B) Last Friday.
(C) Just put it on the desk.

Exercise 22

Where would I find the videos for children?
(A) We made it last weekend.
(B) Where did you last see them?
(C) Look at the end of this aisle.

16. 유흥

Dialogue

Anika : May I help you?

Se-ri : Could you tell me what movies are showing today?

Anika : Today, the showing movies are 'Harry Porter', 'The Lord of the Ring', and 'Mission Impossible 2'.

Se-ri : Which film is popular?

Anika : I'm not sure, but I think 'MI 2' is a good movie if you like action movies.

Se-ri : Do you know the synopsis of that movie?

Anika : Ethan Hunt, performed by Tom Cruise, leads his team on a mission to capture a deadly German virus before it is released by the terrorists.

Se-ri : It sounds interesting to me! Let me have two tickets, please.

Anika : O.K. That will be $14.00.

Key Expression

1. 영화 제목 'Frequency'는 '자주 일어남', '(맥박 등의) 횟수, 도수' 또는 '진동수, 주파수' 등의 뜻이 있다. 'Gladiator'는 '(고대의) 검투사'를 말한다.
2. 'MI 2'는 'Mission Impossible 2'의 약어이다.
3. 'Synopsis'는 '줄거리'를 말하며 'story'라고 표현하기도 한다.

· 실례합니다. 이 자리 임자가 있나요?
(Excuse me. Is this seat taken?)
· 좌석 안내도가 있나요?
(Is there a guide to the seating?)
· 입구가 어디인가요?
(Where is the entrance?)
· 지금 표를 살 수 있나요?

(Can I still get a ticket?)

Word Study

· theater : 극장
· performance : 공연
· stage : 무대
· ticket office : 매표소
· reserved seating : 지정석

Exercise 23

Wasn' t that a beautiful picture he painted?
(A) His camera must be very expensive.
(B) I didn' t like it either.
(C) Yes. He is a very talented artist.

Exercise 24

What are you planning for your vacation?
(A) The plans will be finished by tomorrow.
(B) I am hoping to get to Europe this year.
(C) The weather is really terrible.

Exercise 25

What do you do at the travel agency?
(A) I am in charge of Visa
(B) I work in a large law firm.
(C) Euro Money is better than traveler' s check.

17. 약국 이용

Dialogue

Patient : Can I get my prescription filled here?

Pharmacist : Sure. Can I see your prescription?

Patient : Certainly.

Pharmacist : O.K. It' ll be ready in a moment…. Here it is.

Patient : Does it have any side effects?

Pharmacist : No, not really.

Patient : How and When do I take these tablets?

Pharmacist : Take two tablets after every meal.

Patient : By the way, do you have a medicine for indigestion?

Pharmacist : Let me see. I suggest you take these tablets.

Patient : Thanks a lot.

Key Expression

1. 'fill' 은 여기에서 '(처방을) 조제하다' 라는 뜻으로 쓰였다.
2. 'side effects' 는 주로 'harmful aftereffects' 의 뜻으로 '부작용' 이라고 번역된다.
3. 'indigestion' 은 '소화불량' 의 뜻을 가진 단어로 부정의 의미를 가진 접두사 'in' 과 '소화' 의 의미를 가진 'digestion' 이 합하여 만들어진 단어이다.

· 열이 있는 것 같습니다.
(I have a fever. / I feel feverish.)

· 오한이 납니다.
(I feel chilly.)

· 구토가 납니다.
(I feel like vomiting.)

· 기침이 멈춰지지 않아요.

(I can' t stop coughing.)

· 목이 아파요.

(I have a sore throat.)

· 코가 막혔습니다.

(I have a stuffed nose.)

· 콧물이 납니다.

(My nose is running.)

· 배가 아파요.

(I have a stomachache.)

· 허리가 아파요.

(I have a backache.)

· 온몸이 가렵습니다.

(I feel itchy all over my body.)

Word Study

· 설사 : diarrhea
· 현기증 : dizziness
· 빈혈 : anemia
· 불면증 : insomnia
· 당뇨병 : diabetes
· 폐렴 : pneumonia
· 골절 : fracture
· 신장병 : kidney trouble
· 변비 : constipation
· 부종 : swelling
· 천식 : asthma
· 가슴앓이 : heartburn
· 맹장염 : appendicitis
· 타박상 : bruise
· 자상 : laceration

Exercise 26

What about the company' s no-smoking policy?
(A) I feel great since I quit smoking.
(B) The committee has introduced a new policy.
(C) I think it' s for everybody' s benefit.

18. 물건사기

Dialogue

Saleswoman : Good afternoon, ma' am. What are you looking for?

Customer : I' m looking for a sweater.

Saleswoman : How about this?

Customer : Well. Do you have any other style?

Saleswoman : Let me see. How about this one?

Customer : I like the color. May I try it on?

Saleswoman : Sure. What' s your size?

Customer : I' m not sure. Would you take my measurements?

Saleswoman : O.K. I think the medium size would fit for you. And just a minute. I' ll bring it over.

Customer : Where is the fitting room?

Saleswoman : Let me show you the fitting room. This way, please…. Do you like it?

Customer : It' s too tight. Is there any larger one?

Saleswoman : Sure. Just a second, please…. Do you like it?

Customer : Yes. How much does it cost?

Saleswoman : It' s $54.38 with tax.

Customer : O.K. I' ll take this.

Saleswoman : Cash or charge?

Customer : Charge, please.

Key Expression

1. 'ma' am' 은 여자에 대한 존칭어로 반대로 남자에겐 'sir' 를 쓴다.
2. 'May I try it on?' 은 쇼핑을 할 때 옷이나 액세서리 그리고 신발 등을 입어보거나 신어봐도 되냐고 물어보는 표현이다.
3. 'measurements' 는 복수형으로 쓰여 '(옷의) 치수' 를 말하며 단수인 'measurement' 는 '측

량' 이나 '측량법' 등의 뜻이 있다.
4. 'bring it over' 는 '~을 가져오다' 라는 뜻을 가진 관용어이다.
5. 'the fitting room' 은 탈의실을 말한다.

· 영업시간이 어떻게 됩니까?
(What' s the store' s hours?)
· 다른 것을 보여 주세요.
(Show me another one, please.)
· 좀더 싼 것이 있나요?
(Is there anything cheaper?)
· 포장해 주시겠어요?
(Would you please wrap it up?)
· 배달해 줄 수 있나요?
(Can I have it delivered?)
· 전부 합계가 얼마입니까?
(How much is it all together?)
· 길이를 고쳐줄 수 있나요?
(Would you adjust the length?)

Word Study

· department store : 백화점	· pants : 바지
· wrap : 포장하다	· price tag : 가격표
· Jewelry : 보석류	· fitting room : 탈의실

Exercise 27

What do you think of this terrible heat wave?
(A) I wish the temperatures would fall.
(B) It seems like a bad plan.
(C) They' re very humid.

19. 퇴숙

Dialogue

Guest : Check out please.

Cashier : What' s your room number?

Guest : 707.

Cashier : Are you Ms. Hannah?

Guest : Yes, I am.

Cashier : How was your stay in our hotel? Was everything O.K.?

Guest : Yes, my stay in your hotel has been very pleasant.

Cashier : I' m glad to hear that.

Guest : May I have my bill?

Cashier : Just a second, please. It comes to $135.89.

Guest : Is this the total amount due?

Cashier : Yes, ma' am. How would you like to pay your bill?

Guest : I' d like to pay by traveler' s checks.

Cashier : May I have your passport or ID, please?

Guest : Here you are.

Cashier : Could you sign it here for me?

Guest : Sure.

Cashier : Thank you for staying with us.

Key Expression

1. 'I' m glad to hear that' 이란 직역한다면 '그 얘기를 들어서 기쁘다' 라는 뜻으로 어떤 표현에 대해 긍정적인 반응을 보이는 표현이다.
2. 'total amount due' 란 '지불해야 할 총 금액' 을 말한다.
3. 'ID' 란 영어의 'Identification' 의 약어로 흔히 'Identification Card' 즉 우리말의 주민등록증이나 운전면허증 같은 '신분증' 을 말한다.

4. 이 요금에 세금과 서비스 요금이 포함되어 있나요?
(Does this bill include the tax and service charge?)

· 하룻밤을 더 묵어도 될까요?
(Can I stay one more night?)
· 제 짐을 내려다 주세요.
(Would you take my baggage down?)
· 이 요금은 무얼 말하나요?
(What' s this charge for?)
· 제 짐을 맡겨 주시겠어요?
(Can you keep my stuff?)

Word Study

· tax : 세금
· receipt : 영수증
· refrigerator : 냉장고
· dining charge : 식대
· bill : 계산서
· amount : 금액
· service charge : 봉사 요금

Exercise 28

What are we going to do if the weather gets colder?
(A) We had a lot of cold weather last year.
(B) It' ll get more freezing than this in the winter.
(C) We' ll have to move the event indoors.

Exercise 29

Where can I get tickets for a flight to Taipei?
(A) I understand it' s quite far.
(B) On Monday.
(C) At the window to your right.

20. 귀국 준비

Dialogue 1. 비행기예약 재확인

Travel Agent : Delta Airlines. May I help you?
Su-Yeong : I'd like to confirm my reservation.
Travel Agent : What's your name and flight number, ma'am?
Su-Yeong : My name is Su-Yeung Lee and my flight number is 210.
Travel Agent : Where is your destination?
Su-Yeong : Incheon, Korea.
Travel Agent : Just a moment, please. O.K. Your reservation has been confirmed.
Su-Yeong : Thank you.
Travel Agent : Thank you for using Delta Airlines.

Dialogue 2. 탑승 Check-in

Ticket-issuing Staff : Good evening. May I see your ticket and passport, please?
Passenger : Here you are.
Ticket-issuing Staff : Do you have any baggage to check, Ms. Bush?
Passenger : I have two pieces of baggage.
Ticket-issuing Staff : Did you pack those by yourself?
Passenger : Yes, I did.
Ticket-issuing Staff : Which seat do you prefer?
Passenger : A window seat, please.
Ticket-issuing Staff : Here is your boarding pass and your departure time is 9:30 p.m.
Passenger : Thank you.
Ticket-issuing Staff : You're welcome. Have a good flight.

Key Expression

1. 'confirm' 은 동사로서 '확실히 하다, 확인하다, 승인하다, 굳히다' 등의 뜻이 있다.
2. 'destination' 은 '(여행 등의) 행선지나 목적지' 를 말한다.
3. 'thank you for ~' 는 '~을 해 주어서 고맙다' 는 뜻으로 예로 '알려줘서 고맙다' 는 'Thank you for the information.' 그리고 '도와줘서 고맙다' 는 'Tank you for the help.' 그리고 '시간을 내줘서 고맙다' 는 'Thank you for the time.' 등으로 표현한다.
4. 'pack' 은 여기에서 동사로 '(짐을) 싸다, 꾸리다' 의 뜻으로 쓰였으며 '짐을 본인이 쌌는가' 를 묻는 이유는 혹시 다른 사람이 위험물을 짐 속에 넣을 수 있다는 가정하에 본인이 직접 짐을 쌌는지 여부를 묻는 것이다.
5. 'a window seat' 은 창가 자리를 말하며, '통로 옆자리' 는 'an aisle seat' 이라고 한다.

· 좀 더 빠른 비행 편으로 변경할 수 있을까요?
(May I change my reservation to an earlier flight?)
· 탑승구가 어디에 있나요?
(Where is the boarding gate?)
· 면세점이 어디에 있나요?
(Could you tell me where the duty-free shop is?)
· 예약을 취소하고 싶습니다.
(I' d like to cancel my reservation.)
· 대기인 명단에 올려 주세요.
(Would you put me on the waiting list?)

Word Study

· confirm : 확인하다
· cancel : 취소하다.
· duty-free : 면세
· boarding pass : 탑승권
· carry-on baggage : 기내 반입 수화물

Exercise 30

Will you be traveling first class?
(A) No, my ticket is in business.
(B) No, I' m on my way to Europe.
(C) Even so, I wouldn' t like to fly.

IV

여행항공 용어

IV

PRACTICAL
TRAVEL & AVIATION
ENGLISH

Part IV

glossary

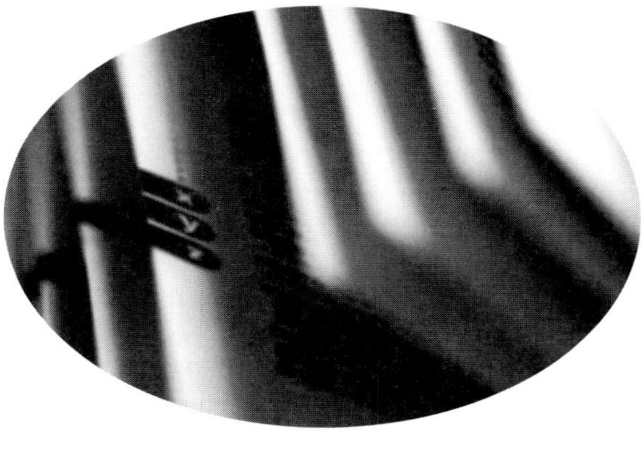

A

aboard	On an aircraft, boat, or other vehicle
accessible	Within reach or easy to get to
accomodations	Food and or a place to sleep
accomodations facility	A place where a traveler can get or sleep
achieve	To gain
activities	The things that people do
adds	Last minute reservations added to the reservation list on the day of arrival
adjoining rooms	Rooms that about along the corridor but do not connect through private doors
admission fee	A charge to enter a place
advance deposit	A deposit furnished by the guest on a room reservation that hotel is holding
advertising	The use of announcement in newspapers, on television, etc., to tell people about a product, service, or personal need
advertising agency	A company that designs, writes, and places advertising in the media
advertising budget	A chart or plan showing how much money is being spent during a specific time on advertising and how much money should result
advertising campaign	A series of paid advertisements designed to produce specific re-sults
affiliated hotel	One of a chain, franchise, or referral system, the membership of which provides special advantages, particularly a national reser-vation system
after departure(AD)	A late charge
agency or agent	A company or person who represents, or acts for, another person or company
aircraft	Any type of machine that files, including airplanes, helicopters, balloons, and gliders
airline	A company that owns and operates airplanes that carry passen-gers and or cargo

airliner	A large airplane owned and operated by an airline
airplane	A flying machine that is heavier than air, is driven by engines, and has fixed wings
airport	A place where aircraft take off and land. It includes all the facilities necessary for taking care of airplanes, passengers, and freight.
air traffic controller	A person who directs aircraft as they are landing at or taking off from an airport and along flight routes between airports
aisle	A passageway, usually between seats
allowance(rebate)	A reduction to the folio, as an adjustment either for unsatisfactory service or for a posting error
altitude	The height above sea level
American plan(AP)	Travel or hotel accomodations that include two or three meals a day
announcement	A speech or a public notice
approach pattern	The way or route an aircraft takes to come to an airport for a landing
arrival card	See immigration card
arrival time	That hour by which the guest specifies he or she will arrive to claim the reservation
artisan	A person who makes handicraft items
ATC(Air Traffic Conference)	A group to which all airlines in the United states belong. It establishes regulations for the airlines and sets requirements for travel agents and agencies.
attitude	A way of thinking or feeling about something or someone
attractions	Beautiful scenery or interesting or historic places that bring tourists to a country
available	Ready for use; when a hotel room is available, it is not occupied by anyone else
average room rate	The average rate paid by guests; computed by dividing room revenue by the number of rooms occupied

B

baggage	The personal property that people take with them on a trip; also called luggage
baggage check or tag	An identification tag for baggage that is checked on a vehicle. It consists of two parts: the strap portion is attached to the luggage; the claim check or stub is used by the passenger to claim the luggage on arrival
baggage compartment	A separate place in a vehicle where baggage is carried
bed-and-board	American plan
bed-and-board house	A guest house that provides breakfast as well as sleeping accomodations
bed and breakfast (B&B)	Lodging and breakfast offered in a domestic setting by families in their own homes; less frequently, the Continental plan
bed night	See guest day
bell captain	A person who supervises bellman
bellman or bellhop	A person who takes guests' luggage to their room and helps them get settled. This person also runs errands and does other things to make guests comfortable.
Bermuda plan	American plan
berth	A bed on a train
beverage	A drink
bills	Paper money
block	A restriction placed in a pocket of the room rack to limit the clerk's discretion in assigning the room; a number of rooms reserved for one group
block book	To make reservations at one time in a group (block) for a large number of airline seats, theater seats, hotel rooms, or other facilities
board	To get on a vehicle
boarding pass	A special document issued at the time of check-in that must be shown as a passenger boards a plane
book	To reserve or hire something or someone

box lunch	A light meal that is packed in a box so it can be taken along to eat while traveling
broadcast media	Radio and television
brochure	A printed folder or pamphlet about a place, product, service, or company that is used for advertising purposes
bus	A large land vehicle that carries many passengers: in a restaurant, to clear a table
bus boy	A person who sets and clears tables in a restaurant
bus stop	The place where passengers wait for a bus
buy in bulk	To buy for large numbers of people at one time

C

CAB(Civil Aeronautics Board)	A government agency that regulates routes and fares of airlines within the United States
cabin attendant	A person who takes care of the comfort and safety of passengers on an airplane; also called flight attendant
caferers	People who cook and supply food for others to serve
camp grounds	Places with special facilities for people who wish to camp
cancellation	A guest' s request to the hotel to void a reservation previously made
captain	The pilot or person in charge of an aircraft or ship
cargo	See freight
car rental agency	A service for renting automobiles for short periods of time
carrier	The airline carrying a passenger on a flight. On tickets, this word is used instead of airline
Carry-on luggage	The things people bring with them onto a plane; also called hand luggage
cash advance	Money disbursed for guests, either advances or loans, and charged to their accounts like other departmental services, also called *cash paid-outs*
cashier	A person who accepts payment for products or services in a restaurant, hotel or store; a person who changes or holds cash, or

	rent
caterers	People who cook and supply food for others to serve
charter	To rent
charter plane	An aircraft that is rented to fly whenever and wherever the person who rents it wishes
checked baggage	Baggage carried in the baggage compartment of the same plane on which the passenger is traveling
check-in	All the procedures involved in receiving the guest and completing the registration sequence
check-out	All the procedures involved in the departure of the guest and the settlement of the account
CIT(Charter Inclusive Tour)	A packaged tour that uses chartered aircraft for transportation
citizenship	Where a person is a citizen, or has political rights and privileges, and, in return, gives allegiance, or loyalty, to the government
claim check	Stub; the part of a baggage check that is used by the passenger to claim the luggage on arrival
class	The type of service on a plane- first, tourist, or economy- depending upon price
clear	To take away dishes from a table
client	A customer; a person who purchases services or products
climb	To move to a higher altitude
cockpit	The pilot's cabin, where the pilot sits to fly the plane; also called flight deck or pilot's cabin
code	A system of numbers, letters, or abbreviated words used to make communication easier. Airlines use letter codes to identify airports, airlines, and types of service.
coffee shop	A restaurant that serves light meals(foods that are simple, easy, and quick to prepare) and snacks(foods eaten between meals)
collect	To get payment for
command	"to have a good command" of a language means to speak and understand it well
commission	A percentage of the price of a sale that is paid to the seller

common language	A language shared by many people from different countries
commuter	A person who travels to work each day. A rail commuter rides a commuter train at special times in order to arrive at work and home at the same time each day.
comp	Complimentary; accommodations–and occasionally food and beverage–furnished without charge
compartment	An enclosed space in which to put things away
compete	To struggle against another person, business, or country to gain something
complaint	Unhappiness or dissatisfaction with products or services
concealed	Hidden
concierge	A French word meaning "doorkeeper" that is used in English to describe a hotel employee who is in charge of special services for guests, such as getting tickets for shows, arranging for local tours, and recommending restaurants and places of interest
conduct a tour	To lead or take people on a tour
conductor	A person in charge of passenger services on a train
confidence	Trust, belief
confirm	To make sure that something will be done or will happen. Airlines ask passengers to reconfirm their flights by notifying the airline that they will use the tickets that were reserved for them.
confirmation form	Proof that a reservation was made
connecting room	Adjoining rooms with direct, private access making use of the corridor unnecessary
consequence	A result
contact or in contact	(To be) in touch with someone
continental breakfast	Coffee and rolls served for breakfast by hotels or other facilities
contraband	An item that cannot legally be brought into or sent out of a country
control tower	The place from which aircraft traffic is directed
convenient	Easy or suitable to a person's needs or comfort; the opposite is *inconvenient*
convention	A meeting at which people, usually in the same business, indus–

	try, or profession, exchange their ideas, experiences, knowledge, etc.
conventioner	A person attending a convention
converse	To talk with
conveyer belt	A continuously moving mechanical device that carries things from one place to another
cooped up	To be confined, or shut up, in one place
cooperate	To work together
copilot	The pilot who assists and relieves the captain during a flight; also called first officer
correspondence	Letters or documents that someone sends and receives
country of origin	The place where someone was born or from which something comes
coupon	A part of a ticket that can be separated from the rest of the ticket. An airline ticket has a coupon for each leg of a flight.
craft	Something that requires special skills to make
crew	All the people who work on the airplane except for the officers
cruise	A pleasure trip by boat
cubbyhole	A small enclosed space that holds messages for hotel guests and their room keys
curb	The edging that protects and separates the sidewalk, where people walk beside the street, from the street
currency	The money of a country
currency exchange	Where the money of one country can be exchanged for the money of another country
customer	A person who buys products or services; client
customs	Taxes charged on things brought into a country. The tax itself is called a duty. When an item is duty free, there is no tax. Customs also means the style of life or traditions of a country.
customs declaration	A statement made or a form filled out by a traveler about things brought into a country
customs inspector	A person who inspects, or examines, luggage and other things brought into a country for contraband (illegal items) or to deter-

mine whether any duty due

D

day coach	A special railroad car for passengers
deluxe	A non-U.S. designation implying the best accommoda- tions
denominations of currency	The names and values of money
depart	To leave
department store	A large store that sells many different kinds of goods in separate sections, or department
departure lounge	An area in an air-port terminal where passengers wait before boarding their planes
departure tax	A special fee that passengers are charged when they leave a country. The money is used to maintain the airport, promote tourism, and train people to work in tourism industries.
deplane	To leave an airplane
depot	Railroad station
descend	To move to a lower altitude
destination	The place to which someone is going
diet	All the food a person eats
dining car	A special railroad car where passengers eat
diorama	A small-sized display or model
diplomat	A person who is tactful and persuasive
direct	To point or show the way to a place; to give directions
directions	Instructions on how to get somewhere
direct mail	Letters, brochures, and other advertising literature mailed to se-lected lists of people
director	A person who manages or leads
discount	A lower price
disembark	To leave a ship or aircraft
disembarkation card	See immigration card
display	To show
document	An official paper that gives information about or prof of some-

	thing
domestic	Within one country
doorman	A person who helps people enter or leave a hotel or other building
double	A bed approximately 54 inches by 75 inches; the rate charged for two persons occupying one room
double occupancy rate	A rate used for tours where the person charge is based on two to a room
downgrade	Move a reservation or registered guest to a lesser accommodation or class of service; cf. upgrade
dresser	A piece of furniture with drawers for clothing
duty	See customs; also, responsibility
duty-free shop	A place where international travelers can buy items without paying taxes on them

E

early arrival	A guest who arrives a day or two earlier than the reservation calls for
economy class	Tourist class; a non-U.S. designation for limited service hotels whose accommodations frequently lack private bath
efficiency	Accommodations that include kitchen facilities
embark	To leave a place. An embarkation or departure card is sometimes filled out by passengers as they leave a country.
embroider	To decorate with specially sewn stitches
emergency	A sudden or unexpected happening that makes quick action necessary
emigration	Leaving one' s country to live somewhere else
employee	A person who works for another person or company
encounter	To meet
en route	On the way
entertainment	Activities that amuse people, such as theaters, amusement parks, etc.

entry-level employee	A beginning employee or worker
escape	To achieve freedom
escort	To accompany or go with someone
European plan	Travel or hotel accomodations that do not include meals
exhibit	Something that is displayed, or shown. Conventions often have exhibits to show products of interest to the people attending.
exhibit hall	A large area or room in which many products can be displayed, or shown
experienced	Having had practice doing something
explore	To look around and learn about a new or strange place
express	A train or bus that makes few or no stops before reaching its destination
extinguish	To put out

F

face down	Facing the table; in a restaurant, a guest check is presented with the items ordered and the prices facing the table
facilities	Places used by tourists for sleeping, eating, meeting, traveling, or recreation
familiarization trips	Free trips offered to people in the travel industry of the media to familiarize, or acquaint, them with a place
family plan	A special room rate that follows children to occupy their parent' s room at no additional charge
fare	The price charged for transportation
farm out	Assignment of guests to other properties when a full house precludes their accommodation
fatigue	Tiredness
feeder lines	Airlines that connect smaller cities and towns with each other or with major cities and airports
file	A group of records or similar documents that are kept together in some order so that they can be found easily. Also, a cabinet or drawer that holds these records or documents.

first-aid	Help or treatment given to a hurt or sick person before regular medical treatment from a doctor can be obtained
first officer	Copilot; the pilot who assists and relieves the captain during a flight
flight	A trip by air
flight attendant	Cabin attendant
flight deck	Cockpit
flight engineer	A pilot whose responsibilities include the operation of the engine and other mechanical equipment of the aircraft during a flight
formal	Following certain rules of dress and behavior; the opposite is *informal*
franchise	The right to operate a business. When a hotel or restaurant is a franchise, the operator has to run the business according to certain standards set by the company that rents or sells the franchise. The operator pays a percentage of the earnings, or income, to the company.
free day	A day during a tour when no activities are scheduled
freight	Goods or products carried on vehicles; also called cargo
freight train	A train that carries freight
front desk	In a hotel, where guests register, or check in
fuel consumption	The amount of fuel being used
fuel flow	The speed at which fuel is going from the gas tanks to the engine and is being used
full house	100 percent occupancy, all guest rooms sold
full service	A complete line of services and departments are provided, in contrast to a limited service hotel or motel

G

galley	A small kitchen on a plane, boat, or train, where food can be cooked or made ready to be served
gate	The entrance to a terminal; the airport area at which flights arrive and depart and the point at which passengers can leave or

	board their flights; also the entrance to the tracks where people can board a train
general manager(GM)	The hotel' s chief executive
getting away	Escaping; going on a vacation; leaving on a trip; leaving to return home
gift shop	A store that sells presents, or gifts, things that people give to others
grandmaster	House emergency key; one key that opens all guest rooms except those locked from within
graveyard	A work shift beginning about midnight
ground transportation	Buses, taxis, cars, etc., that take people from the airport to their destinations
guaranteed reservation	Payment for the room is promised even if the occupant fails to arrive
guest check	A slip of paper on which menu items that the guests order are written, together with their prices. When the check is totaled, the waiter or waitress adds up all the prices, including any taxes, for the guest to pay.
guest folio	A form with several parts that contains information about hotel guests and a place to record charges and money paid
guest house	A house in which a few rooms are rented to tourists for sleeping; also called tourist home
guest ledger	A section of the guest folio on which all charges and money paid by a guest are entered. It is used by the hotel for billing and accounting
guide or tour guide	A person who leads tours and tells people about the places of interest
guidebook	A book that tells about an area, including the places of interest and how to get to them
guide tour	A tour, often for sightseeing purposes, that is accompanied by a guide

H

handcart	A small vehicle, usually two wheeled, that is pushed by hand and

	is used for carrying things such as luggage
handicraft	Something made by hand that requires a special skill, usually done in the custom or tradition of a country
hand luggage	See carry-on luggage
heading	The direction in which an aircraft is moving
hobby	An activity done for relaxation
hospitality	The quality of making people feel welcome and comfortable; hotels and restaurants are often called the hospitality industry
host or hostess	A person who welcomes, or greets, guests and makes them comfortable by taking care of their special needs; in a restaurant, the person who shows people to their table and gives them menus
hostel	An inexpensive type of accommodation for tourists who are on hiking or bicycle trips
hotel chain	A corporation that owns and operates many hotels
hotelier	French for innkeeper
housekeeper	A person who supervises cleaning and making up rooms for hotel guests
hydraulic system	All equipment on airplanes operated by the pressure of liquids

I

IATA(International Air Transport)	A voluntary association of international airlines that sets fares and other standards by agreement for most airline service
immigrant	A person who enters a country intending to stay permanently
immigration	Entering a country for the purpose of living there
immigration card	An information card that a person entering a country is asked to fill out; also called arrival or disembarkation card
import	To bring a product into a country for the purpose of selling it there
impression	A feeling or an idea
incentive (group)	Persons who have won a hotel stay as rewarded for meeting and excelling their sales quotas or other company-established standards
inclusive terms	Phrase that is sometimes used in Europe to designate the Ameri-

	can plan
income	Money received for services or products
independent traveler	A person who travels on his or her own rather than a member of a group
induce	To persuade someone to do something; to bring about or cause something to happen
inducement	Something that persuades or influences people
influence	To change someone's thinking or behavior without using force
in-season rate	High season rate; a resort's maximum rate, charged when the demand is heaviest, as it is during the middle of the summer or winter; cf. off-season rate
inspector	Supervisory position in the housekeeping department responsible for releasing on-charge rooms to ready status
institutional advertising	Advertising intended to keep the name of a company or country before the public without giving information about any particular products or services
intention	A plan
intercom	A wired system of voice communication between rooms or other nearby areas in which each station, or place of communication, has both a microphone and a speaker; also called an intercommunication system
interline connection	A connection, or change, from one airline to another
internal tourists	People who travel within their own country
international class tourism hotel	A hotel that has all the facilities needed to accommodate internal tourists
IT(Inclusive Tour)	A packaged tour that offers transportation, accommo- dations, and sometimes sightseeing tours with transportation usually on scheduled airlines, although some may be by bus or train
itinerary	A listing of route and, or activities during a trip

J

jet plane	An airplane with engines that provide a propelling force by dis-

	charging heated gas from the rear of the engine
junior suite	One large room, sometimes with a half partition, furnished as both a parlor and a bedroom

K

keyed up	Excited, tense, or restless
king	An extra long, extra wide double bed about 78 inches by 80 inches

L

labor-intense	Having a high proportion of workers as compared to the number of people served
landing	The action of an aircraft when it arrives and sets down on the ground
landing gear	The mechanism that lowers the wheels of a plane and on which a plane lands
late arrival	A guest with a reservation who expects to arrive after the cutoff hour and so notifies the hotel
late charge	A department charge that arrives at the front desk for billing after the gust has checked out
leg of a flight	One part of an entire trip that a person is making by air
license	A document that gives a person or a business permission to carry on a particular kind of activity
limousine	A large automobile that carries many passengers
linen closet	A storage closet for linens and other housekeeping supplies usually located conveniently along the corridor for the use of the housekeeping staff
linen room	The housekeeper' s office and the center of operations for that department, including the storage of linens and uniforms
literature	Any printed material used for advertising or promotion
lobby	A room or hallway at the front of a building through which people enter the main part of the building. In a hotel, guests register

	and are greeted in the lobby. Guests can also wait for and visit with friends in the lobby.
local	A train or bus that makes many stops; also, the immediate area
local lines	Feeder lines; airlines that connect smaller cities and towns with each other or with major cities and airports
local tour	A trip to see the sights of an area
locate	To find
locomotive	A train engine
log	A record of activities maintained by several operating departments
lost and found	An area, usually under the housekeeper' s jurisdiction, for the control and storage of lost-and-found items
long-haul route	Long-distance transportation
lucky	To have good fortune, to have things go well or smoothly
luxury item	Something people having but do not need

M

maintain	To keep in good condition
management contract	An agreement by which the builder of a hotel allows another company or person to manage and operate the hotel. Each gets a share of the earnings. Large hotels built by governments are often operated in this way.
manager	The person in charge of a business
marina	A place where boats can dock and people can use their boats for accommodations
market	The people who will buy a particular product or service or visit a particular place; also, a place where things are sold
master account	One folio prepared for a group(convention, company, tour)on which all group charges are accumulated
media	A plural word referring to all the ways of spreading information, such as newspapers and magazines(print media) and radio and television(broadcast media). *Medium* is the singular and refers to

	each of these means individually.
memories	The mental reminders of people, places, things, or experiences
menu	A listing of the items served in a restaurant and their prices
merchandise	Goods or product; anything sold by a store
merchant	A person who sells things
mezzanine	An extra floor between two other floor. It is usually a balcony or part of it is the mezzanine
modified American plan(MAP)	A method of quoting room rates in which the charge includes breakfast and dinner as well as the room
monument	Something set up or built in memory of a person or event; a building or structure that survives from a past age
morning call	A wake-up telephone call made by the telephone operator at the guest's request
motel	A hotel with special facilities for automobiles or motor vehicles
motor coach	Same as bus
motorist	The driver of an automobile
Ms	An abbreviation used to indicate a female guest whose marital status is unknown
multiplier effect	The number of times that money from tourism is spent within a tourist destination area
Murphy bed	A standard bed that folds or swings into a wall or cabinet in a closetlike fashion

N

national	A person who is a citizen of a country either by birth or by sewing allegiance and becoming a citizen
native	A person who is a citizen by birth
news release	An Article written to be given out to the media as free advertising
nickname	A short, familiar way of saying someone's name
night auditor	A person who works at the cashier window in a hotel during the late night and early morning hours. This person brings the guest

	accounting records up-to-date, or makes them current up to that time.
nonscheduled airline	An airline that operates on routes and at times according to demand for service rather than following a timetable
non-transferable	Something that cannot be used by any person except the one to whom it is issued or whose name is on it
no-show	A reservation that fails to arrive
notice	To see, to observe
notify	To report a fact or tell someone about something

O

occupancy rate	The percentage of rooms or beds that are occupied at a certain time or over a period of time
occupied	Being used; when something is not occupied, it is *unoccupied*
off season	A time when tourists do not come to an area either because of whether conditions or because it is not usual vacation time
on change	The status of a room recently vacated but not yet available for new occupants
origin country	The place where a tourist was born or from which the tourist comes
out of order(OOO)	The room is not available for sale because of some planned or unexpected shutdown of facilities
over and short	A discrepancy between the cash on hand and the amount that should be on hand
overbooking	Committing more rooms to possible guest occupancy than are actually available
overhead compartment	An enclosed space in which to put things that is located above the heads of the airplane passengers
overstay	A guest who remains beyond the expiration of the anticipated stay
overweight	In describing baggage, weighing more than is allowed

P

pack	To put things in a suitcase or box; to take things out is to *unpack*
package tour	A tour offered by a travel agency or an airplane that includes the cost of hotels and sightseeing as well as the cost of transportation. It may also include transfers and meals. The cost of air transportation on a package tour is usually much lower than regular fares.
party	The number of people who will occupy a hotel room
passenger	A person who travels in an airplane, train, boat, bus, or automobile
passenger service agent	A person who works at an airport whose job is to help passengers while they are on the ground
passenger train	A train that carries people
passport	A document issued by a country ti its own citizens that gives them permission to leave and then reenter the country
PBX	Private branch exchange; a telephone switchboard
pension	A type of accommodation that offers bed and breakfast at low prices
penthouse	Accommodations, usually suites, located on the top floor of the hotel
pilot's cabin	Cockpit
port	A place where ships unload cargo or let off passengers
porter	A person who carries things for others
preassign	Reservations are assigned and specific rooms blocked before the guest arrives
prepay	To pay in advance, or ahead of time
press conference	A meeting attended by members of the media for an announcement of interest to their readers or listeners
press release	A news story for use by media as free advertising
print media	Newspapers and magazines
professional writer	A person who makes his or her living through writing

project	To make guesses, or to estimate, in advance
promotion	A part of an advertising campaign that is aimed at pushing, or developing, a particular product, place, or service
propeller plane or prop	An airplane that has conventional internal combustion engines and propellers, or revolving blades, that push or drive the plane
psychologist	A person trained to understand peoples' thoughts, emotions, and behavior
public address system	Part of an intercommunication system that has a loud- speaker, making it possible to speak to many people at the same time. The people who are listing over such a system cannot communicate with the person speaking unless they are also using the inter-com. Public address systems are used in airports or on planes to make announcements.
publicity	Something that is brought to the attention of the public; often, free advertising or a news release that appears in newspapers or magazines
public relations	The business of making contact with the public to establish a good attitude on its part toward a place, product, or service
qualify	To become more fit, as for a job

Q

qualify	To become more fit, as for a job
queen	An extra long, extra wide double bed about 60 inches by 80 inches
quote	To state the room rate or other charges

R

rack	Room rack; a piece of front office equipment representing the guest rooms in the form of metal pockets in which colors and symbols identify the accommodations
radar	A device that sends out radio waves in a beam. When reflected back from a distant object, the beam indicates the position, dis-

	tance, and direction of movement operates trains
rate of exchange	The value of one country' s currency as compared to another
recline	To lean back
recommend	To tell good things about a person, place, or thing
reconfirm	To verify that a reservation will be used
recycled	Reused
refill	To fill again
register	To record or note something, such as a guest' s arrival at a hotel
registration	Check-in
regulation	A rule
repeat business	The business that comes from satisfied customers who return to buy more of a product or service
represent	To take the place of and act for another person or company
reservation	A room or a seat that is being held another person or company
reserve	To save or hold something, such as a room or seat, for someone
resident	A person who lives in a country but may be a citizen of another country
resort	A place that provides recreation and entertainment for vacations. A resort hotel has these facilities on its own grounds for its guests.
resources	All the natural and manufactured wealth of a place or country
retail	Describing a business that sells directly to the public, a retail travel agency acts for the public in arranging for and buying transportation, accommodations, and other travel services
revenue	Income, money received
room a guest	To take the guest' s luggage to the room and help the guest get settled
room count	The number of occupied rooms
roomette	A small room on a train where passengers can sit during the day and sleep at night
rooming(a guest)	The entire procedure by which the desk greets and assigns new arrivals and the bell staff directs them to their rooms

rooming list	The list of names furnished by a buying group in advance of arrival and used by the hotel to preregister and preassign the party
room rack	A rack that contains spaces into which cards are placed to show the status of hotel rooms. There is one space, or slot, for each room
room service	A catering service that brings food and beverages to a guest' s room in a hotel
round trip	A trip on which the passenger returns to the starting point
route	The way transportation moves between two places
rude	Not courteous, not polite
runaway	A cleared strip or area on which an aircraft can lead or take off
rural area	A farm or country area

S

safe-deposit boxes	Individual sections of the vault where guests store valuables and cashiers keep house bank
sales per occupied room	Average room rate
schedule	A list of things that will happen in the order of when they will happen. For transportation, a schedule, or timetable, lists the times of departure and arrival; also, to schedule an activity means to reserve a time for doing that activity.
scheduled airline	An airline that operates on fixed routes and at fixed times, according to a timetable
seat belt	A safety belt, or strap, that fastens a person to the seat of an airplane, automobile, etc., to protect the person from being tossed about by bumps or jolts
sector	A part or section
security check	An examination of passengers and their carry-on luggage for concealed weapons, usually using x-ray equipment and metal detectors.
security officer	A person who conducts a security check

segment	A part of something
self-contained	To have all the facilities and accommodations needed by tourists in one hotel or area, such as at a resort
semiskilled worker	A person who does work that does not require much training
seniority	The length of service or the amount of time a person has worked for a company
serve	To be useful; to take care of; in a restaurant, to provide food or a meal; to serve an airport means provide serve by flying aircraft in and out of that airport
service charge	A percentage(usually from 10 percent to 20 percent) added to the bill for distribution to service employees in lieu of direct tipping
short-haul route	Short-distance transportation
shoulder	Marketing term designating the period between peaks and valleys; the time on either side of the in-season
siberia	Jargon for a very undesirable room, one sold only after the house fills and then only after the guest has been alerted to its location or condition
sidewalk	A place where people walk beside a street; it is separated and protected from the street by a curb
sightseeing tour	A trip to see the sights of an area
sightseers	People who go to places of interest to see the sights
single	A bed approximately 36 inches by 75 inches; a room with accommodations for one; occupancy by one person; the rate charged for one person
skill	The ability to do something well because of training, practice, or experience. A person who does a job that does not require much training and skill is a semiskilled worker; a person doing a job that needs no training of skills is an unskilled worker
skipper	A guest who departs surreptitiously leaving an unpaid bill
sleeper	A departed guest whose room rack slip remain in the rack giving the appearance of an occupied room
sleep out	A room that is taken, occupied, and paid for but not slept in
sleeping car	A railroad car where people can sleep in berths, compartments

	that open up to become beds
smuggler	A person who tries to brings into a country without paying duties or who brings in contraband items
snack	Food eaten between meals
social director	A person at a resort or hotel or on a cruise ship who is in charge of activities to amuse and entertain the guests
source	The place from which something comes
souvenir	Something that helps to bring back memories
spread rate	Assignment of group members or conventioneers using the standard rate distribution, although prices might be less than rack rates; cf. run-of-the-house rate
stable	Remaining the same, as a rate of exchange
stall	An enclosed space in a market or an exhibit hall where things can be displayed
staple	The main part of a diet
statistics	Groups or totals of numbers telling about things
stay over	An anticipated checkout who remains beyond the stated date of departure; any guest who remains overnight
steward or stewardess	A man or woman who is a cabin or flight attendant
stow	to put something away
strap portion	The part of a baggage check that is attached to the luggage
suite	A series of connecting rooms with one or more bedrooms and a parlor; suites occasionally include additional rooms like a dining room
supervise	To be in charge of the work of other people and to make sure it is done properly
support facilities	Things that are necessary for the operation of tourism facilities, such as roads to airports and hotel, electricity, sewers, water supply, etc.
swing	The work shift between the day shift and graveyard shift, usually starting between 3 p.m. and 4 p.m.

T

takeoff	When an aircraft leaves the ground
taxiing	The movement of an airplane on the ground at an airport
taxi strip	Runaway along which an airplane moves on the ground
tenant	A person who rents
terminal	The beginning or ending place for aircraft, trains, buses, and other forms of transportation. It is also the building where facilities are provided for travelers and baggage. It can also be a place in the city where passengers check in for a flight and get transportation to the airport.
ticket	A receipt for payment for transportation that allows people to fly or ride on a vehicle; a receipt that allows admission to movies, theatrical shows, etc.
ticket agent	A person who represents a company by selling tickets that allow the purchaser to use the company's transportation
timetable	A schedule that shows at what time a vehicle will arrive at and depart from the various stops along the route. Airline timetables also give the type of aircraft, frequency of service, meal service, and other information.
tip	The money over the cost of the service that is given as thanks to the person who performs the service. Some services, such as those of porters, are performed only for tips.
toiletry items	Things such as soap or toothpaste used in washing or grooming oneself
total check	To add up all the prices of the items ordered
tour operator	A company that owns or rents equipment of facilities and provides services for special travel arrangements or activities for tourists
tour packager	A company that puts together the facilities and services of tour operators, transportation companies, accommodations facilities, and amusement or entertainment facilities as tour packages to be sold to the public through retail travel agents

training	The instruction for some job or work
transcontinental	Across one continent
transfer	The handling and transportation of baggage to and from airports. This service is often included in packaged tours.
transient guest	A short-term guest
transoceanic	Across the Atlantic or Pacific Oceans
transportation	The carrying, or taking, of something or someone from one place to another
travel agency or agent	A company or a person who acts for someone in making travel arrangements
trunk line	an airline that operates between major cities or airports
turn away	To refuse walk-in business because rooms are unavailable; the guest so refused
turn-downs	An evening service rendered by the housekeeping department, which replaces soiled bathroom linen and prepares the bed for use
turn-in	The sum deposited with the general cashier by departmental cashier at the close of each shift
twin	A bed approximately 39 inches by 75 inches to sleep one person

U

unaccompanied baggage	Baggage that does not travel on the same plane as the passenger
understay	A guest who checks out before the expiration of the anticipated stay
upright position	The most forward position of an airline seat
up-to-date	Current or completed up to the time the action is taken

V

vacancy	Occupancy of less than a full house so rooms are available for sale

vacation	A holiday; time off from work or other duties
validate	To make something legally binding or official. Before an airline ticket can be used for transportation, it has to be validated by the ticket agent, who stamps or writes on it that payment was received.
valet service	Cleaning, laundering, or repairing of guests' clothing
vehicle	Something that moves and carries passengers or freight
verify	To make sure that something is correct
visa	A travel document that gives permission for a foreigner to enter(and, in some cases, to leave) a country. It is a special endorsement, or written approval, that is usually stamped in a traveler's passport.
volume	A large amount; a tour packager works in volume by making reservations for many travelers at the same time
voluntary	Of one's own choice
vouch	To agree to be responsible for someone else or for what someone else says or does
voyage	A trip

W

waiter or waitress	A man or a woman who serves food in a restaurant
walk-in	A guest without a reservation who requests and receives accommodations
welcome	To greet kindly and gladly, to show or receive someone with hospitality
wholesale	Describing a company that sells to other companies or to retailers, who sell directly to the public
word-of-mouth advertising	Recommendations of satisfied customers who tell others about a place, product, or service

외항사승무원 영어 필기시험 _ 예제 1

* Read the following passage and answer the questions.

Do plants grow better if we talk to them? No one knows for sure. many scientists think that sound can affect plants. soft and (1) music seems to help them grow better. Loud music with drums seems to kill them. But plants can't understand words, so saying nice things to a plant should not affect it's growth. Still, some scientists claim that plants react to the feelings of people's (2) and even in their thoughts. They say that plants grow better if we think nice thoughts and they "faint" or even die if we think nasty thoughts. But other scientists don't believe that this is (3). (4) Many people have done experiments to find out if they are true. So far everyone has (5) come up with a different results

1. Select the most suitable word for (1).

A. bright B. reliable C. quiet D. simple E. loud

2. Select the most suitable word for (2).

A. words B. musics C. songs D. thoughts E. emotions

3. Select the most suitable word for (3).

A. false B. likely C. absurd D. true E. good

4. Translate the underlined sentence (4) in to korean.

5. Select the word or phrase that has the same meaning as (5) come up with.

A. imagined B. made up with C. thought over
D. prepared E. arrived at

* Encircle the correct forms.

6. Supposing your mother (sees, saw, seeing) you, what would she say?

7. The man didn't attend the meeting. (or, nor, but) did I.

8. That was the first time (when, which, that) I met him.

9. We must always keep our hands (clean, cleaned, cleaning).

10. Whenever I see this picture, I am reminded (by, of, for) my grandparents.

외항사승무원 영어 필기시험 _ 예제 2

* Read the following passage and answer the questions.

Oscar Wilde, an Englishman, arrived at New York to undertake a lecture tour. The reporters who saw him on the ship were a little disappointed by his appearance, which was more like that of a sportsman than an artist. He had long hair, and he wore a dark green overcoat, with a round cap on his head, but he was a giant in stature and his hands looked terrible. Wilde naturally expected them to ask him about his work. But they asked him how he liked his eggs fried, What he slept in, how he cut his fingernails, and what temperature he liked his bath to be. His answer showed a lack of interest in the questions.

The passenger, therefore, began asking more questions one after another. They heard him complain that the trip was dull, that the ocean did not roar, and that nothing less than a storm which swept the bridge from the ship would give him any pleasure. That was enough for the reporters, who told their readers that Wilde was "disappointed with the Atlantic Ocean," a phrase which got him far more publicity than his views of art would have done.

1. Oscar Wilde's voyage to new York was not pleasant because ______________

A. he got seasick.

B. he was surrounded by many passenger.

C. he had to answer many silly questions.

2. The people on the ship found him ______________

A. greatly different from what they had imagined.

B. somewhat different from what they had imagined.

C. exactly the same as they had imagined.

3. The people were disappointed because Wilde ______________

A. was carrying a dark green overcoat.

B. was a sportsman.

C. looked like a sportsman

4. The people questioned Wilde ______________
A. about his health.
B. about how he spent the days on the ship.
C. about what he had never expected.

5. The passengers asked many questions because Wilde ______________
A. was talkative.
B. was not interested in the reporters' questions.
C. answered all the questions readily.

6. Wilde answered the questions ______________
A. eagerly.
B. angrily.
C. halfheartedly.

7. Wilde told the passengers that the Atlantic Ocean was ______________
A. not pleasant to cross.
B. stormy.
C. hardly seen form the ship.

8. The reporters told the readers that Wilde was ______________
A. not pleased with the Atlantic ocean.
B. disappointed with the Americans.
C. an artist rather than a sportsman.

9. The reporters news ______________
A. made Wilde famous immediately.
B. made Wilde hated by the Americans.
C. told about Wilde' s view of art.

10. The people were interested in ______________
A. Wilde' s view of art.
B. Wild' s transatlantic trip.
C. the Atlantic ocean.

외항사승무원 영어 필기시험 _ 예제 3

* Read the following passage and answer the questions.

A green I−538 form is used by international students in order to obtain permission from the Immigration and Naturalization Service to transfer from one university to another in the United States. If you are planning to transfer, remember that you must obtain permission before leaving the university where you are currently studying. You must complete the form I−538, have it signed by a foreign student advisor, and submit it to the District Office of the Immigration and Naturalization Service together with the form I−20 from your new school and the small white form I−94 that was affixed to your passport when you entered the country. Submitting the signed I−538 and other documents does not insure permission to transfer. Only an official of Immigration can decide such a case. Students who have not completed one term of study at the school that issued them their first I−20 are not advised to file for permission to transfer until they have completed one term.

1. A transfer form is called an ___________.

A. I−20　　B. I−94　　C. I−538　　D. I−520

2. If you want to transfer it is a good idea to ___________.

A. travel to the new university immediately so that the foreign student advisor can help you

B. study at the university where you have permission until you receive new permission form Immigration

C. sign an I−538 form and leave it at your current university before traveling to the new university

D. leave the country so that you can enter on another I−20 from the new university

3. In order for you to transfer, permission must be granted by an official at the ___________.

A. foreign student advisor' s office　　B. new university

C. Immigration office　　D. passport office

4. The transfer form must be signed by the __________.

a. foreign student advisor at the new school

B. foreign student advisor at the currents school

C. Immigration officer

D. student

5. The word insure in line 9 means __________.

a. confuse B. deny C. guarantee D. sign

* Read the following passage and answer the questions.

Do you often dream at night? Most people do. When they wake in the morning they say to themselves "what a strange dream I had! I wonder what made me dream that?" Sometimes dreams are frightening. Terrible creatures threaten and pursue us. Sometimes in dreams, wishes come true. We can fly through the air or float from mountain-tops. At other times we are troubled by dream in which everything is confusing. We are lost and nothing can' t find our way home. The world seems to have been turned upside down and nothing makes sense.

In dreams we act very strangely. We do things which we would never do (1). We think and say thing we would never think and say. Why are dreams so strange? Where do dreams come from? People have been trying to answer this since the beginning of time. But no new has produced a more satisfying answer than a man named Sigmund Freud. One' s dream-world seems strange and unfamiliar, he said, because dreams come from a part of one' s mind which one (2). He named this the "unconscious mind." Sigmund Freud was born about a hundred years ago. He lived most of his life in Vienna, Austria, but ended his days in London soon after the beginning of the Second World War. Freud was one of the great explorers of our time. But the new worlds he explored were (3). The unconscious mind is like a deep well, full of memories and feelings. These memories and feelings have been stored there from the moment of our birth- perhaps even before birth. Our conscious mind has forgotten them. We do not suspect that they are there until some unhappy or unusual experience causes us to remember, or to dream dreams. Then suddenly we see a face we had forgotten long ago. We feel the same jealous fear and bitter disappointments we felt when we were little children.

This discovery of Freud' s is very important if we wish to understand why people act as they do. For the unconscious forces inside us are at least as powerful as the conscious forces we know about. Why do we choose one friend rather than another? Why does one story make us cry or laugh while another story doesn' t affect us at all? Perhaps we know why. If we don' t, the reasons may lie deep (4).

6. Select the most suitable word for (1).

A. when we are awake
B. once we are ready
C. before it is too late
D. because it mean work

7. Select the most suitable word for (2).

A. has easily touched and felt
B. is willing to interfere with
C. can neither recognize nor control
D. will see better with a microscope

8. Select the most suitable word for (3)

A. not known in Vienna
B. going to disappear soon
C. inside man himself
D. regarded as useless

9. Select the most suitable word for (4).

A. in the history of explorations
B. in our unconscious minds
C. in children' s dream worlds
D. in our joys and fears

10. (5) "what is dream?"

A. Terrible monsters chase you in most dream.
B. A dream has a lot to do with our memories and feelings.
C. Every dream a wish that has come true.
D. A dream makes it harder to live one' s real life.

11. (6) "why do we suddenly remember something we had forgotten long ago?"

A. We sometimes dream, and we experience strange things in dreams.
B. Children forget things easily but adult remember them.
C. The memory has always been there in the unconscious mind.
D. We remember something when our mind' s well is full.

정답 예제 1

1. C 2. D 3. D 4. 많은 사람들은 그것들이 사실인지 알아내기 위해 실험을 했다.
5.E 6. sees 7. nor 8. when 9. clean 10. of

정답 예제 2

1. C 2. B 3. C 4. C 5. B 6. C 7. A 8. A 9. A 10. B

정답 예제 3

1. C 2. B 3. C 4. B 5. C 6. A 7. C 8. C 9. B 10. B 11. C

참고문헌

1. Gerson, Steve. et al. *On the Go. Hong Kong*: Longman Asia ELT, 2004.

2. Gerson, Steve. et al. *On the Move. Hong Kong*: Longman Asia ELT, 2004.

3. Wajnryb, Ruth. *Travel and Tourism*. Tokyo : MACMILLAN, 2000.

4. 제천, 단양, 영월, 평창군청 홈페이지

5. 대한항공 홈페이지

6. 각국 화폐는 http://keb.pe.kr에서 퍼옴

7. 우리말 고유명사는 문화관광부 고시 제2000-8호 "국어의 로마자 표기법"에 따름

여행항공 실무영어
PRACTICAL TRAVEL & AVIATION ENGLISH

1판 1쇄 발행 2011년 2월 28일
1판 2쇄 인쇄 2013년 2월 12일
1판 2쇄 발행 2013년 2월 22일

지은이 구헌철 이필만
펴낸이 윤용호
펴낸곳 順學堂
121-868 서울시 마포구 신수동 448-6
등록 2001.10.23. 제10-2238호
전화 02)719-6116
팩스 02)719-6120
www.shdbooks.co.kr
E-mail: shd6116@chol.com

ISBN 978-89-93158-36-6 93740
가격 15,000원